Gerald Loren Fishkin, Ph.D.

FIREFIGHTER
AND PARAMEDIC
BURNOUT

THE SURVIVAL GUIDE — THE ROLE YOU PLAY

Also By Gerald Loren Fishkin, Ph.D. :

POLICE BURNOUT
Signs, Symptoms and Solutions

FIREFIGHTER
AND PARAMEDIC
BURNOUT

THE SURVIVAL GUIDE – THE ROLE YOU PLAY

Gerald Loren Fishkin, Ph.D.

Published by

HBJ HARCOURT BRACE JOVANOVICH
Legal and Professional Publications, Inc.

Distributed by
LAW DISTRIBUTORS
14415 South Main Street, Gardena, CA 90248
(213) 321-3275

Library of Congress
Cataloging in Publication Number: 88 – 064150
ISBN: 0 – 15 – 630950 – 5

Printed in the United States of America

First Edition
August, 1989

ACKNOWLEDGMENTS

This book has been, for me, a journey that few outside the day to day life of firefighters and paramedics ever experience. It has taken me into their inner world of grief, understanding, and human compassion that could not have been imagined, understood, or written about without the assistance of a deeply caring team of professionals of the very highest caliber. My gratitude is extended to the following individuals who played a significant role in the actualization of this work:

To Mr. Meyer Fisher, Senior Vice President, Harcourt Brace Jovanovich, Legal and Professional Publications, Inc., my mentor, for his support and belief in the value of this project from the outset, and whose deep understanding of the human condition led to this author's clarification of the concept of burnout as well as providing me with the title of this work, I offer, as my humble *quid pro quo*, my deepest gratitude and respect.

To Craig B. Kelford, II, my technical editor, whose insight, courage, and encouragement was the impetus that led to this book becoming a reality, my eternal thanks.

My secretary, Tiffany A. de Ruosi, provided flawless word processing skills and profound patience and enthusiasm in the preparation of the manuscript and index, including the transcription of dozens of hours of on-the-scene interviews.

My thanks to Mr. Larry Kuzela for masterfully editing the final manuscript and maintaining the consistently high level of organization and presentation of my work.

To Ken Welling of Image Masters, Laguna Beach, California, my appreciation for his exquisite implementation of the overall design and electronic typesetting of the final manuscript, including the cover layout.

For providing me with the most recent data regarding firefighter work illness and injury data, I gratefully acknowledge the assistance of The International Association of Firefighters, Washington, D.C., Mr. Kevin O' Gara, Research Analyst, State of California, Division of Labor Statistics and Research, David L. Christianson, Manager, Public Agency Contract Services, California Public Employees' Retirement System, Mark J. Gerlach, Insurance Consultant, and Glenn M. Shor, California Policy Seminar, University of California, Berkeley.

For permission to quote from copyrighted material, my sincere thanks to Mr. A.C. Bushnell, Publisher, Executive Health Report, The American Psychiatric Association, and, Alfred A. Knopf, Inc., for permission to quote from How Can I Help, by Ram Das and Paul Gorman.

To Kathy, my wife and best friend, for all of the days and nights spent alone while I was away doing the field research for this book, and then patiently coping with my own irrationality while I was putting it all together, my deepest love.

Finally, to the many fire departments who so generously opened their doors to me, and most important, to the dedicated firefighters and paramedics who shared their experiences with an unparalleled sense of openness to this relative stranger, my everlasting appreciation and respect.

— For Kathy —

CHAPTER TWO

DEALING EFFECTIVELY WITH FIREFIGHTER STRESS

CHAPTER THREE

ANXIETY

CONTENTS

INTRODUCTION

CHAPTER ONE

THE DYNAMICS OF FIREFIGHTER STRESS

". . . *facing suffering continuously is no small task. We learn the value of recognizing our limits, forgiving ourselves our bouts of impatience or guilt, acknowledging our own needs. We see that to have compassion for others we must have compassion for ourselves.*"

Ram Das and Paul Gorman

CHAPTER FOUR

DEPRESSION

CHAPTER FIVE

THE DYNAMICS OF CRISIS

CHAPTER SIX

FIREFIGHTER BURNOUT

CHAPTER SEVEN

ALCOHOLISM AND THE FIREFIGHTER

CHAPTER EIGHT

ORGANIZATIONAL CONTRIBUTIONS TO FIREFIGHTER STRESS

CHAPTER NINE

STRESS AND RETIREMENT

POSTSCRIPT

THE FIREFIGHTER BURNOUT SYNDROME

INDEX

INTRODUCTION

The commonly held perception that public safety personnel are invincible, and are able to handle community safety and security needs without absorbing the adverse effects of repeated exposure to a negative environment, is a myth. The result is the alarming rise in the number of stress-related emotional and physical disorders among today's firefighter population.

The primary purpose of this book is to illuminate the signs and symptoms of firefighter stress and to suggest effective methods for preventing burnout from becoming a reality.

This book is for the firefighter under stress, and for his family members and peers. Fire administrators will gain a clearer perspective regarding symptoms of stress among subordinates as well as organizational factors which contribute to or exacerbate employee stress. Finally, therapists will benefit from an understanding of the firefighters' unusual work environment, its effect upon them and their families.

DEFINITION OF FIREFIGHTER

For our purposes, the term firefighter refers to those professions which are a part of, or supplementary to, the profession of the working firefighter. These include: Emergency Medical Technicians, Paramedics, Flight Nurses, Ambulance Drivers, Medevac Pilots, Lifeguards, and highly specialized disaster personnel such as Earthquake Heavy Rescue teams.

I have taken the liberty of altering the use of masculine and feminine pronouns to allow for ease of reading, and no sexist bias is intended. Also, this writer makes no pretense to cover all events or stressors confronting firefighters in their personal and occupational life.

THE FIREFIGHTER'S WORK ENVIRONMENT

The regular work environment and role expectations of today's firefighter are *unusual* at best. The emotional and physical stresses which firefighters are exposed to are often constant and unremitting. Through a process of negative conditioning, like developing an allergic reaction, we often become adversely sensitized to our own work place. In a sense our work setting becomes *psychonoxious* for us. Our work environment can become as toxic to our emotional system as chemicals can be to our body.

Firefighters' work expectations require rapid decision making, and they generally do not have enough time to decompress or recharge between calls. Their unusual work environment is often uncontrollable. Emergency conditions and time constraints are the rule rather than the exception. Firefighters know at some level that they have maximum responsibility and minimum control. Thus, frustrations are constant and coping requirements are enormous.

For the stressed firefighter, the work place begins to become *noxious*. An environment where it is not just the increasing frequency of stressors or demands, but rather the duration that begins to erode their spirit.

As internal pressures increase, the stressed firefighter becomes anxious at just the thought of going to work.

Anticipation that was once full of excitement becomes one of dread, anticipatory anxiety, and ultimately emotional exhaustion and depression.

The constant sense of emotional pounding begins to wear on the tiring firefighter. As the sense of frustration becomes unremitting and turns to anger, *burnout has begun to take over*!

MISCONCEPTIONS ABOUT BURNOUT

The term *burnout* is popularly used to describe a feeling of frustration with one's environment. To this extent, burnout is frequently perceived to be something other than total exhaustion of the individual's ability to cope with stressors. There is also a general opinion that burnout can be remedied by getting more sleep, taking a vacation, or simply changing one's attitude. Hence, society sees those who are no longer able to perform their jobs as weak or simply not trying hard enough. In reality, the firefighter suffering from clinical burnout has no choice about continuing in his profession, and, in addition, must also make fundamental changes in his life. Thus, the objective is to avoid burnout at all cost.

Burnout is not dramatic, but rather a slow, insidious process that takes its toll in many ways. The loss of personal and spiritual values, which relate to meaning and purpose in life, is a primary result of the burnout syndrome. Based upon clinical experience, burnout is complete; loss of occupation generally results. Burnout can be, and usually is, a financial drain to the disabled firefighter, his family and his employer. The employer must ultimately pay wages for a lifetime of services not received when a firefighter enters into early retirement as a result of burnout. Thus, if burnout can be avoided or averted, everyone benefits.

STRESS IN THE WORKPLACE

It is a fact that psychological disorders among workers in both the public and private sectors are one of the fastest growing categories of occupational disability claims in this decade. According to the National Council on Compensation Insurance, stress—related injuries now account for roughly 14% of all occupational disease claims, up from less than 5% in 1980.[1] During 1988, benefit payments for mental problems increased 27% nationally over the preceding year.[2]

The International Association of Firefighters (IAFF) Annual Death and Injury Survey[3] is a primary source of

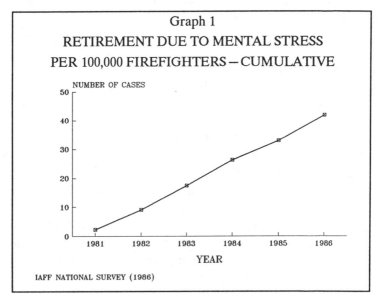

Graph 1
RETIREMENT DUE TO MENTAL STRESS
PER 100,000 FIREFIGHTERS — CUMULATIVE

NUMBER OF CASES

YEAR

IAFF NATIONAL SURVEY (1986)

national data regarding occupational diseases among firefighters. The IAFF Survey data includes retirement rates for firefighters suffering from all occupationally disabling diseases, including mental stress. Graph 1 presents the national cumulative increase of mental stress claims resulting in disability retirements among our nation's firefighter population between 1981 and 1986.

While no single source of data may accurately reflect the true incidence of occupational illness among firefighters today, several types of data collected in California may be compared for assessing the extent of the problem.[4]

California leads the nation in the total number of stress-related work injuries and disability retirements. A large-scale report prepared for the County Supervisors Association of California[5] indicated that between 1980 and 1988, occupational injury claims for mental stress among

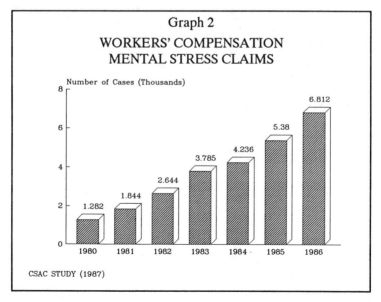

Graph 2
WORKERS' COMPENSATION
MENTAL STRESS CLAIMS

Number of Cases (Thousands)

CSAC STUDY (1987)

public sector employees increased *five-fold*. This dramatic increase in occupationally related mental stress claims is presented in Graph 2.

Of the 58 counties sampled in the above study, data indicated that 11% of all county government indemnity cases were attributed to stress. Of interest is that these cases represented almost 30% of the *total* dollars spent on workers' compensation claims. The cost to the insurance carriers or self-insured cities was almost *$70 million dollars* in benefits paid. This growth is particularly alarming when compared to the growth of all other workers' compensation claims. There has been a definite shift in occupational health problems away from acute effects toward chronic effects of toxic exposures, and reactions to stressful working conditions.[6] As shown in Graph 3, the number of physical injuries as a percentage of the work force is actually declining.[7]

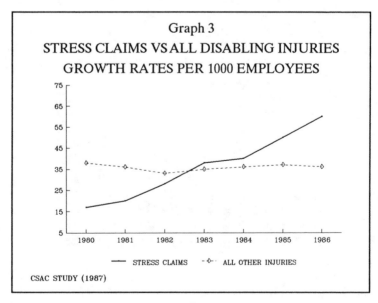

Graph 3
STRESS CLAIMS VS ALL DISABLING INJURIES
GROWTH RATES PER 1000 EMPLOYEES

—— STRESS CLAIMS   -◇- ALL OTHER INJURIES

CSAC STUDY (1987)

According to the California Department of Industrial Relations,[8]   the fastest growing area of disabling illness reported by all employers is "anxiety reactions and mental disorders." These disorders have increased 756%, from 796 cases reported in 1977, to 6,812 cases in 1986.[9] In the public sector, teachers, police officers and firefighters filed the majority of stress-related disability claims.

Thus, data collected by state government and labor unions alike validate the grim reality that occupational diseases due to stress-related factors are significantly on the rise. What irony, the professionals that protect and educate us also suffer the most from their work! Additionally, at both state and national levels, systematic tracking of psychologically hazardous work exposures has been neglected.

INADEQUATE EVALUATION OF OCCUPATIONAL STRESS

The problem of evaluating the extent of occupational stress is hampered by the fact that out of approximately 500,000 qualified physicians in the United States today, only 800 are board-certified in occupational health. Thus, ". . . most workers with work-related medical problems receive treatment from physicians who have little or no training in occupational health."[10] Work-related stress conditions are most likely counted inaccurately since the general practitioner is unfamiliar with the psychologically and physically negative effects of the firefighters work environment.

Unfortunately, there is no uniform reporting of data on

a state by state basis regarding the incidence of firefighter occupational stress or retirements resulting from factors of stress. Estimates of occupational illness, which have not yet become disabling enough to become workers' compensation cases, are similarly ambiguous.[11]

THE FIREFIGHTERS' DILEMMA

The nemesis of work life today for most firefighters is that the effects of their work shift overflow into the leisure or recreational aspects of their life. Hence, everything becomes a duty, a responsibility. Ultimately, the stressed-out firefighter begins to see survival itself as a responsibility, a duty, a chore!

The firefighters' occupational world is steeped in tradition, which, as many associated with it know, is slow or reluctant to change. Yet, change it must, in order to accommodate to the growing needs of its employees regarding early stress detection and management.

The role of the firefighter in contemporary society has changed dramatically from its original design and intent. Coupled with changing role expectations are the ever increasing effects of stress and burnout.

FIREFIGHTERS — PAST VERSUS PRESENT

In decades past, a firefighter primarily fought fires and occasionally performed difficult rescues. On any particular day, a firefighter might have averaged from one to six calls.

Firefighters of the past trained, cleaned the station,

inspected buildings for fire hazards, and did a significant amount of firefighter education work within their community. Depending on their station's socio-geographic location, firemen may have slept through the night on a consistent basis. However, most of their time was spent waiting for the bell to ring.

The firefighter of today has a much different job description. The work day consists of a much different emphasis. They respond to many more calls, sometimes over twenty per shift. Approximately 80% of these calls are *Medical Aid Incidents*. The firefighter is also concerned with a new danger, that of personal liability for his job efforts.

There is a fire department axiom which says, "If there is a problem and you don't know who to call, call the fire department." Community members have responded to this new perception of the fire department in that they will call if anything is out of the ordinary in their life. The fire department receives calls for many non-emergency medical problems; from an individual's inability to relieve himself, to helping someone get into their own bed. Sometimes the community has recognized that the fire department responds faster than do other public safety personnel, hence, they will first call upon the fire department for help in any threatening situation.

In all, today's firefighter not only has a tremendously stressful job as he deals with sickness, trauma, and death, on a regular basis, but also feels the potential threat of administrative reprisal and possible legal action if his behavior is not above reproach.

In days past, firemen simply put out fires. Today, they

are also emergency medical experts, and somewhere in the process of helping others, many become cynical, disillusioned, emotionally and physically exhausted, and occupationally dysfunctional.

Occupational disability is devastating. It is painful and costly. Often, the employer is oblivious or reluctant to address the emotional needs of the employee. This is especially true in the world of today's firefighter.

References

1. *Wall Street Journal*, 7 April 1988.

2. *Wall Street Journal*, 21 February 1989.

3. International Association of Firefighters, Department of Occupational Health and Safety. *1986 Annual Death and Injury Survey.* Washington, D.C.: International Association of Firefighters, 1986.

4. Shore, Glen M. *Occupational Disease Compensation In California.* Berkeley: California Policy Seminar, Research Report, University of California, 1987.

5. County Supervisors Association of California. *Stress Related Disability Retirements, A Special Report Prepared For The Assembly Public Employees, Retirement And Social Security Committee .* Sacramento: County Supervisors Association of California, 1987.

6. Shore, Glen M. *Occupational Disease Compensation In California.* Ibid., IX.

7. County Supervisors Association of California. *Stress Related Disability Retirements.* Ibid., 3.

8. California Department of Industrial Relations, Division of Labor Statistics and Research. California *Work Injuries And Illness.* San Francisco: Division of Labor Statistics and Research, 1987.

9. Ibid., 1977–1987.

10. Levy, Barry, "Occupational Health in the United States: Its Relevance to the Health Professional," in *Occupational Health*, ed. Barry Levy and D. Wegman. (Boston: Little Brown, 1983), 6.

11. Shore, Glen M. *Occupational Disease Compensation In California*. Ibid., 21.

CHAPTER ONE

THE DYNAMICS OF FIREFIGHTER STRESS

We have to take the value judgments out of stress.
GLF

During the last decade, newspaper and magazine articles have heightened our awareness of the occupational hazards of firefighter work. Motion pictures and television have also sensationalized the dynamics of today's firefighter. We are led to believe that firefighters are superhumans who never tire of responding to any emergency with a helpful smile and a true concern for the public's best interest. Firefighters are depicted in the media as happy-go-lucky public relations experts. Their occupation is characterized as appreciated, and one in which exciting and rewarding rescues happen daily. More realistically, however, the occupation of firefighter is one of responding to routine calls, whose repetition is reflected directly by the civic nature of their response.

In economically depressed areas, the firefighter supplements the role of the personal physician by treating "emergencies" such as colds, cramps, coughs, and other ailments. Yet, the same emergency call might require the firefighter's expertise in the treatment of more traumatic injuries, such as stabbings, shootings, and assaults.

In general, individuals who enter the profession of firefighter do so because they have an inherent desire to help people in need. They have an idealistic belief that they are going to save lives on a call-by-call basis, and, *make a difference in society.*

For a growing number of younger firefighters today, after the newness of the job begins to wear thin, many of these dedicated individuals begin to feel as though they are production line machines, rarely having to think, analyze or be creative in the performance of their daily activities.

Firefighters experiencing the effects of occupational stress begin to identify, and become one, with the misery and human pain they see during their day-to-day work. They become hardened and angry, stressed by the lack of sleep and trauma, disillusioned by what they originally set out to do in life, versus how they now feel: tired, empty, emotionally depleted, and often, fearful.   The present becomes heavy and burdensome, the future uncertain.

Reflective of the growing incidence of occupationally related-stress disorders, is the fact that stress-related claims among firefighters and police personnel have increased significantly within the past several years. These claims are now five times greater than disability claims within the private sector. Thus, public safety personnel are five times more likely to suffer a stress-related injury sometime during their career, as compared to workers in the private sector.

The rapidly increasing number of occupational stress claims among firefighters attests to the fact that occupational stress injuries are just as valid as "accidental" physical injuries. Both injuries handicap an employee from effective job performance. In reality, the *normal* working conditions of firefighters are unusual or extraordinary at best.

In the following account, a paramedic with ten years experience, sums up the conflicting occupational and emotional demands which exist in the firefighter's world:

Pulling up, you immediately sense the panorama of confusion. The blue Chevrolet van sits with its driver door open, parked in the middle of the street, askew to the center line. Its lights are still on but the engine is turned off. There are short skid marks.

The engine company is at the scene. A fireman is bent over the broken body of a seven-year-old boy. A crowd of residents have assembled, and a few citizens are pushing the driver up against the back doors of the van. The driver is crying his mistake and disbelief.

Our headlights illuminate the situation and we exit the ambulance. There is a demand made to take the boy to the hospital. The demand is accentuated by a kick to the back of the fireman who is assessing the young boy. There are no police present yet.

Someone has run to notify the mother of the boy. She arrives just as we are retrieving our medical boxes from the rig. She is screaming "Oh God, Oh God!"

The firefighter has had enough of the kicking, picks up the boy and rushes to the ambulance, holding the boy's neck as still as possible.

The boy is placed in the back of the ambulance where the trauma is visible. The fireman has blood on his hands and all over his turn-out pants. The stretcher becomes immediately soaked red in the area of the boy's head. Cries of "Oh shit, this is a bad one" come from the firefighter's mouth.

The boy's head is obviously deformed on the right side. There is blood matting his black hair, and small specks of white material are mixed with the blood. This is grey matter. The rich protein smell permeates the enclosure of the ambulance. The young boy begins to gurgle and shake. His right pupil is fixed and dilated. His right elbow is fractured and his wrist bone is also exposed.

The decision to "scoop-and-run" is made. A quick call is made to the hospital, an initial patient condition is relayed, and an ETA of 1½ minutes is given.

The paramedics and firefighters start to work. A blood pressure is taken while an I.V. is started. One medic attempts an unsuccessful E.T. tube placement. There is some discussion as to the protocol of such an attempt on a child.

We leave the scene, while the angry crowd is punching the driver of the van and the captain of the engine company is trying to control them. As we turn the corner the police arrive on scene.

By the time we reach the hospital the boy is posturing. We unload the gurney and run it into the trauma room. There are at least ten people waiting. As we unload the boy onto the hospital's gurney, his clothes are cut off and his airway is taken over by the respiratory technician. I decide to stay and watch but know nothing is to be learned, so I leave the room and start writing a report. All of a sudden, there is a stillness in the trauma room. The boy is officially dead.

While I am talking to our dispatcher he breaks the conversation and says, "Can you take on a heart at 244 West Broadway?" I say, "Why not?"

||||||||||||||||||||||||||||||||||||||||||||||||||||||||||||||||||||||||||||||||||||||||||||||||||||||||||||||||

While the foregoing example is not representative of all firefighter runs, it does, however, capture the irony present in the work-life of the firefighter; of the necessity to function calmly in the face of human crisis and suffering, while also dealing with the practical aspects of the job.

FIREFIGHTER STRESS AS A PRESUMPTIVE DISORDER

Firefighter stress, in many cases, falls within the category of "Presumptive Disorders". By definition, presumptive disorders are occupationally related illnesses or disabilities that are presumed effects of the job and may not be visible on X-ray or validated by any other objective methods typically used for assessing physical injury or disability. Stress—related disorders primarily comprise the majority of illness found within this category because its effects cannot be seen objectively. Rather, stress is a condition subjectively experienced by the individual.

The presumption of psychological injury further specifies that the disabling condition either manifests itself or develops during employment. This is especially critical if the employee is seeking a stress—related disability retirement and the employer is defending, with the often used counterclaim, that a pre-existing personality or psychological disorder was responsible for the employee's disability.

To disprove a stress claim, employers generally must prove that an employee's stress disorder was caused by something other than the job. In this regard, employers are sometimes relentless in their pursuit to uncover aspects of the employee's life that would be damaging to the disability claim. Such investigation involves explicit details of the firefighter's personal life including use of drugs, alcohol, tobacco, emotional stability and health history of his family of origin.

STRESS — A WORKING DEFINITION

At the most basic level, stress is psychological and is the direct result of the ways in which we have learned to cope. It is a specific emotional and bodily response that is triggered by our perception of signals in our environment or in our thinking.

It is important to distinguish between "stress" and "strain" as is done in physics. Stress may be considered the outside force, strain the reaction of the object under stress. Our personality is the critical variable that alters strain, or our reaction to stress. Thus, the more stable the personality of the individual under constant stress, the less he will be affected by the stressor.

Contrary to popular belief, not all stress is undesirable. In fact, we all experience some level of stress throughout our daily lives, a feeling of tension that is ever-present in this world of many demands and pressures. However, when our internal defense system begins to break down and our coping methods become ineffective, our internal sensation of stress reaches painful proportions and we **must** re-evaluate the manner in which we think, act, and react. Otherwise, the stresses of daily life will surely take their toll.

We owe our basic understanding of stress to the late Hans Selye, M.D., Ph.D.,[1,2] who devoted the greater part of his professional career researching stress clinically, as well as in the laboratory.

Dr. Selye's pioneering work, "STRESS: The Physiology and Pathology of Exposure to Stress"[3] electrified the scientific world through his revolutionary three-phase concept of stress coping. Dr. Selye's extensive laboratory findings conclusively proved that *stress is the nonspecific response of the body to any demands made upon it*. Personal conflicts, marital problems, alcohol and drug use or abuse, and psychological conflicts cause us to employ coping mechanisms to resolve or readjust ourselves; that is, to regain a sense of balance or control over our life situation. Likewise, the reverse is also true, in that maladjustive behaviors often result from trying to cope with other perceived stressors in our life, such as work-related concerns or problems.

Stress is any demand, either internal, external or both, that causes a person mentally and physically to readjust in order to maintain a sense of balance within his life. Thus, stress is not simply nervous tension or anxiety. It must be emphasized that what determines a person's effectiveness on the job, or in daily life, is the way in which he copes with these demands, on both a conscious and subconscious level. The subconscious level consists of automatic responses (psychological defense mechanisms) that protect us emotionally from experiencing psychological pain, such as anxiety or guilt.

Stress is neither "good" nor "bad"; it is simply the result of how we have learned to cope. And, as a chain is only as strong as it's weakest link, so too is the body. As adrenaline pumps into our system, signaling that we must do something to ward off a perceived stressor, body tissue begins to break down, resulting in headaches, ulcers, cardiovascular and neuro-muscular disorders, as well as many other physical and mental conditions.

The effects of stress coping are cumulative, and ultimately result in an attack upon the weakest or most vulnerable part of an individual's body. These effects are different for each person, depending upon the inherent weakness in one's physical or emotional makeup.

This concept of stress becomes much simpler to comprehend when looked at from the standpoint of what Dr. Selye has termed *The General Adaptation Syndrome* (GAS), or biologic stress syndrome. Plainly stated, the GAS is comprised of three stages[4] related to any demand placed upon us, those being:

The Alarm Stage — A person becomes aware of a specific demand or signal requiring a response. It is during this stage that the body begins to secrete adrenaline while the alarm is on. This "adrenaline pump" reaction that is triggered during the Alarm and Resistance phases of the General Adaptive Syndrome creates an instantaneous level of high activation that prompts a person to do something to turn the signal off. The adrenal rush which is experienced is much like the euphoric effect created by coffee, cigarettes or amphetamines. However, the downside of any "high" that results from adrenaline in the bloodstream is the chemical depression that follows when the "high" is over. This is especially true when the Alarm and Resistance phases of GAS are terminated. Additionally, the greater the suddenness, novelty, or ambiguity of a situation, the greater is the potential for stress.

The Resistance Stage — The learned mental and/or physical response to whatever it is in the environment that, requiring a reaction, grabs a person's attention during the Alarm Stage. The manifestations of the second phase are quite different from, and in many instances, the exact opposite of those which characterize the Alarm Reaction. During the Resistance Stage of coping, our learned psychological and physical defense mechanisms are called up to deal with the demand or stressor which is perceived to be a threat to our sense of well-being. Dr. Selye found that with repeated exposure to a noxious agent or stressor, an individual's acquired defenses become weakened and ultimately rendered ineffective in combating stress.[4] Since adrenaline continues to circulate throughout our body during this stage of coping, our behavior **must** be effective in turning off the adrenal response. If unsuccessful, research subjects were found to enter a third stage, the stage of exhaustion. If coping behavior is effective, stage three is automatically bypassed or averted.

The Exhaustion Stage — If our attempts to cope with the perceived demands or stressors continue to be ineffective, and our psychological and physical defenses are just not adequate, psychological and physical exhaustion sets in. The final effect of human exhaustion is death. However, for purposes of the present illustration, exhaustion is equivalent to what we will term "Burnout": *the total inability to maintain a sense of personal balance because learned methods of coping have broken down - are no longer effective in warding off the effects of stress.* Firefighter burnout results when the individual becomes physically, mentally and emotionally incapable of performing the duties and functions of his occupation. At this level, the individual is beyond the point of stress. He is totally dysfunctional and, most often, his burnout affects all aspects of his life. Frequently, this results in depression and often manifests itself in physical disorders as well.

During the stages of Alarm and Resistance, the individual attempting to adjust to internal pressures of a stressor often experiences one or more of the following feelings:

- Anxiety
- Depression
- Low frustration tolerance
- Hostility bordering on hate or rage

Both anxiety and depression, as stated above, result from the effects of the adrenal process operating on our system in such a way as to cause the emotional roller coaster often experienced by firefighters after a shift is over. During the work shift, and especially at night, the excessive consumption of caffeine, cigarettes and sugar (poor coping methods) often adds to the stress on one's system which results in the need to "come down" from the chemical high. Alcohol is often used to aid in the coming-down process. Unfortunately, alcohol is a chemical depressant which further adds to one's stress rather than helping to neutralize or overcome it. Furthermore, repeated efforts to cope with unremitting stress reduces one's ability to deal effectively with frustration. Our tolerance for dealing effectively with frustration is significantly reduced, and, if continued, results in hostility or rage (additional internal pressure) which must somehow be vented in order to reach a sense of balance.

SIGNS AND SYMPTOMS OF STRESS

In order to identify the signs and symptoms of stress, the following list has been compiled from hundreds of case histories of firefighters, paramedics and other public safety personnel who were treated for stress. Also, it is my hope that should these symptoms become apparent, either in the behavior of a firefighter, a loved one, or a peer, that every effort be made to utilize one of the many interventions discussed, in order to avoid the unforgiving effects of chronic stress or burnout.

- Excessive weight gain or loss in a short period of time
- Combativeness, irritability, impulsiveness, hostility, frustration, especially with patients, doctors, nurses, peers, and "top brass"

- Excessive perspiration
- Incident where the life of the patient or firefighter is threatened; and the firefighter shows either no emotion, or an exaggerated sense of despair
- Increased response times
- Excessive use of sick leave when there is no apparent illness (often related to alcoholism and fatigue)
- Frequent use of alcohol or prescribed medications, such as Valium, Librium, Atarax, Elavil, or other prescription medications
- Marital and family disorders including, but not limited to, extramarital affairs, divorce, physical abuse of spouse and/or children, serial monogamy (multiple relationships outside the marriage)
- Sexual dysfunction including impotence, premature ejaculation, need for immediate one-sided sexual satisfaction, low or absent sexual desire
- Mental confusion
- Inappropriate display of emotions when a more rational or compassionate approach may be more appropriate
- Exaggerated fears about personal health or potential job-related injury
- A job-related injury that disrupts the regular work schedule
- Frequent or infrequent complaints of physical distress, including but not limited to, stomach problems, heart disease, PAT (paroxysmal atrial tachycardia), hyperventilation, lower back pain, non-specific musculo-skeletal pain, diabetes
- Unusual number of close calls while responding to an incident

- Frequent complaints regarding personal financial condition
- Excessive notoriety as a result of effective job performance may be symptomatic of a need for attention, acceptance, or a venting of aggression in a socially acceptable way through one's work
- Tremor of extremities, especially while at rest
- Nail biting
- Verbalized feelings of isolation and/or alienation from others, e.g., "Nobody understands me!"
- Overcompensation and arrogant behavior (macho, John Wayne syndrome). Generally covers up an inadequate personality, and often reveals a low threshold for frustration; becomes angry often
- Personality breakdown including disorientation for person, place, or time. May show regressive behavior, often signals the beginning of emotional breakdown. "Crying excessively is not uncommon"
- Impairment in one's ability to distinguish between subjective feelings and objective reality
- Loss of interest in work, family, hobbies, or people in general
- Excessive use of tobacco or other stimulants, including but not limited to coffee and tea
- More than the usual number of "accidents", including vehicular and other types of personal injury. Even Sigmund Freud declared, "Accidents don't happen, they are caused!" May imply unconscious or conscious motivation to remove one's self from the perceived stressor
- Acute or chronic fatigue
- Insomnia and other disturbances of sleep, including nightmares and stress dreams

● Alteration of "normal" work patterns and habits

HISTORICAL ROOTS OF THE COPING PROCESS

Looked at from the standpoint of coping with perceived demands made upon us, stress may then be seen as the outcome of maintaining balance and organization in our life. This is not unique to firefighter work, for every one of us has developed our own specific ways of coping with demands placed upon us, ways in which we interact with others and define ourselves. This coping process has its roots in the early developmental history of the individual. It is determined by how we saw our significant others (fathers, mothers or other important role-models) deal with situations in their own lives.

One of the most important aspects of coping is how adequate the individual believes he is in terms of his capability of dealing with external demands. That is, how one perceives a situation or stressor, and one's perceived ability to cope with the stressor. Again, this is a learned personality pattern rooted in our earliest experiences and role-models.

If there was no adequate male role-model, either due to death, divorce, the father's lack of interest in the family unit, the father's own work demands, or some other reason, this absence often results in poor identification of male role expectations and lack of a secure emotional base from which to draw during times of excessive stress. Males growing up in this type of environment often develop a stereotype of expected "masculine" responses. This creates a basic conflict, in that the male, through his stereotypical thinking, believes he must not show his downside emotions, and as a result, suffers a sense of detachment from his own core of emotional meaning and experience. This also has a profound effect in the interpersonal life of most firefighters.

More often than not, firefighting personnel experiencing stress-related disorders, act in such a way as to cause a relationship to end, either through fear of relating, defensiveness, or general feelings of inadequacy. And yet, girlfriends and extramarital affairs abound in the clinical picture of those firefighters treated for stress. There appears to be a need to be seen as powerful "Paragods" and in control.

PSYCHOLOGICAL ASPECTS OF STRESS

Research and clinical experience are beginning to show that stress is psychologically based rather than the result of one's fear of bodily injury. In fact, we can use the analogy of comparing stress to the demands made upon a battery which supplies light, heat or sound to a system. Regardless of what system is used, if the energy is not replenished in an effective and consistent manner, the battery will soon be drained with no energy left to operate the system. The system then ceases to function at all.

In general, I have found that it was not specifically the role requirements of firefighter that created "stress" in his life, but rather, a combination of factors, primary among these are:

- The personality of the individual, including low self-esteem and the need for recognition
- The unrealistic expectations which the individual brings to the job, especially his perceptions regarding his role as *savior*

- The ability to deal effectively with frustration, especially if one is also undergoing individual or family problems or crisis
- The manner in which the individual deals with authority figures — especially the "brass" at work
- The individual's ability to communicate, primarily regarding emotional issues

From the factors listed above, it should become apparent that for firefighter personnel in general, *the most important stressors are psychologically based and emotionally related* — especially those causing severe distress. There is a strong correlation between our perception of events and the unique ways in which we react to them which result in the mental and physical drain on our system, i.e., stress. In addition to the personality characteristics of those drawn toward a career as a firefighter, and their effectiveness in coping with the demands placed upon them, there are also occupational factors that are unique to the firefighter profession. These factors significantly interact with the personalities of individuals engaged in this type of work.

Following is a summary of those factors found to be of primary importance in the lives of firefighters treated for stress-related disorders. Inherent in any understanding of firefighter stress, and the modification of those stressors, is an awareness of the significance that these forces play in the day-to-day lives of firefighter personnel and their relationship to the frustrations frequently experienced by these individuals.

OCCUPATIONAL FACTORS RELATED TO FIREFIGHTER STRESS

- The frustrations related to dealing with fire administration hve frequently been reported as a primary source of stress among firefighters.

- Personality conflicts occur within a department such as between command staff and their subordinates or with outside agency personnel such as doctors or those involved with the process of county or state certification.

- Firefighters frequently feel that they are in a double-bind in that they are civilly as well as criminally liable for a mistake or misdeed while working. They also face disciplinary action within the organization.

- Firefighter recruits generally believe that their work is primarily that of saving lives. That is just not the case. Community service and routine paperwork, station maintenance and training actually account for approximately 85% of all active firefighter work. There is a general public misconception regarding firefighter work as always being exciting, dangerous, and heroic. Often, nothing could be further from the truth. As a seasoned Battalion Chief stated, ". . . firefighter work is like being a pilot; we may have hours of boredom punctuated by moments of stark terror!"

- The belief that "people should appreciate me" often leads to a firefighter's feelings of resentment, anger, bitterness, vindictiveness, and sometimes hatred, when these expectations are not met.

- Bipolar thinking creates significant continuing frustration leading to stress. Firefighters often perceive things as either "black" or "white" — good or bad; seldom a shade of gray. This type of thinking creates "psychological boxes" of acceptability and unacceptability which are inconsistent with normal or healthy psychological functioning, yet are appropriate in the mechanical nature of firefighter work.

- Over-identification with the "savior role." Often, the firefighter's sense of self as the one doing the job becomes confused with the role of "firefighter." This ultimately results in poor self-identity on the job as well as away from it. Peer reinforcement has a strong influence on this role-identity confusion.

- Pressure to conform to peer group expectations often leads to feelings of alienation and isolation from the peer group when firefighters diverge from the norm and express their own individuality.

- Firefighters function within a paramilitary system. It is inevitable that for many who need to function within the confines of a defined organizational structure, as though it was a surrogate family unit, the captain/chief often represents a symbolic father figure to those subordinate to him. Subordinates many times act out primitive psychological needs representing the ambivalence (combined feelings of love and hate) felt in their own families of origin, especially if they grew up without a male role-model present. Thus, organization, communication, morale, discipline, and professionalism are profoundly negatively influenced.

- Firefighters are often taken for granted by the

general public, and even though it is toward their occupational role, they often have difficulty separating others' reactions to them from who they are as individuals.

- Always dealing with the traumatic side of life at work creates or reinforces one's belief that the whole world is that way. This type of thinking leads to the over generalization that trauma is as much a part of their off-duty world as it is during their work shift. The thought of impending trauma enters into the interpersonal life of the firefighter affecting his relationships with significant others. Firefighters with families are often over-protective of their children as a result.

- Economic and racial prejudice may develop against the people with whom the firefighter comes into contact during their shift.

- Inability to cope with the physical demands of the job is a prominent perception among firefighters who work while injured or are physically out of shape, and are aware of the downside risks related to their lack of physical fitness.

- In general, firefighters are expected to maintain a professional standard in line with the perfection only attributed to the saintly. Mistakes could cost a life. The expectation of perfection dictated by the medical community and fire department supervisors often result in significant feelings of frustration in that no one can live up to these expectations and function effectively.

- The 24-hour shift worked by firefighter personnel creates a strain not only on the firefighter physically, but also causes problems within his family unit as well. Sleep patterns become disturbed as a result of such shift work. Firefighters often sleep during their days off and thus lose contact with the day-to-day activities and needs of their own families, thereby creating additional pressures and frustrations that are counter-productive to a healthy work and home life.

- Firefighters are frequently witnesses to some of the most horrifying aspects of life. Many firefighters deal with this occupational reality through the subconscious psychological defence mechanism of *depersonalization*. This is expressed in behavior through a splitting of one's self emotionally as a means of detaching ego from the job, as if at times you feel as though you're "someone else," or detached from the activity you're involved with. This often automatic form of psychological defense serves to protect firefighters from reacting emotionally while performing their job. While the process of depersonalization is carried out through a form of role-playing, even after the shift is over, the role continues to be played, especially with spouse and family. Another outcome of depersonalization is that firefighters remain further detached from communicating their downside emotions. The negative side of this process is the development of loss of self and increased levels of frustration, since firefighters believe there is no acceptable way to vent emotionally what they actually feel or experience. Anger, rage, or depression are most often substituted for the expression of all other emotions.

- Firefighters tend to be over-spenders, living well beyond their means. This may be seen as a way of overcompensating for a lack of meaningfulness or purpose in their lives, especially as their level of stress coping increases. Spending money also represents a form of power and control, a reality firefighters deal with on such a regular basis that it becomes part of their "firefighter personality," and acted out in their day-to-day interaction with others. Buying "toys," which is a form of competitiveness, serves as a socially acceptable distraction from having to deal with their deeper level emotions. It also keeps them in financial debt, which is also common among firefighters. Most often, firefighters have second jobs, just to help make ends meet. This can add to an already stressful situation for the firefighter. Many times they are working on their days off rather than recuperating for the next shift.

• Fire departments are often notorious rumor mills that perpetuate a sense of "living in a fishbowl." Firefighters often feel an invasion of their privacy by their peers and administrators.

• Firefighters tend to be very competitive, and failure of attaining a promotion at an anticipated time may result in a sense of alienation from the group, including feelings of depression and a reinforced sense of low self-esteem.

• Instantaneous decision-making in the face of definitive administrative guidelines for on-the-spot role performance adds to the double-bind experience and frustration.

• Training and station assignments that are not challenging or seen as not important by the firefighter are viewed as a waste of effort and add to a sense of loss of purpose and meaning.

- Firefighters often work diligently to save a life and later find that the patient had died or the system did not further support the patient's right to life. This often adds to significant occupational frustration and emotional overload.

- Female hospital personnel are an ever-present reality in the world of firefighters. Females are especially drawn to paramedics who symbolically represent safety, security, and emotional strength. The potentiality of developing personal relationships with members of the opposite sex as a result of professional contact through one's occupation can threaten all aspects of a firefighter's life. This is especially true if the firefighter is vulnerable due to already present marital and or family problems, or if his self concept or self image is in need of an ego boost.

- Fire station interpersonal relationships have a great deal to do with stress in the firefighter's life. Because of the many hours the crew is together, relationships can grate on one another, and can result in a voluntary or involuntary transfer to another station.

- The firefighter's work schedule produces stress in that it is generally out of synchrony with the schedules of non-firefighter friends and other relationships. Firefighters tend to associate of-duty with other firefighters with similar schedules thereby creating a closed system of interaction with the "outside world."

- There is stress in protracted idleness in that many firefighters are assigned to locations where there is little or nothing to do or relatively few calls per day (sometimes averaging less than one per day). Firefighters assigned to these slow stations must be of a psychological makeup compatible with a lack of motivation, otherwise stress will develop. Many times the firefighters working at the slower stations have been assigned there in order to recuperate from being over stressed, traumatized, physically limited, or in a pre-burnout condition. Most people would consider having a 24-hour period in which to do relatively little to be a luxury, yet many firefighters faced with this reality become disappointed in their occupation. They question their purpose and contribution to the department. They are concerned about their skills becoming dull. Some firefighters adapt well to the slower station assignments in that they have outside interests or hobbies that they bring with them to work. Others become television addicts. While still others become stressed with the vast amount of time they have on their hands. They become indulged in self thought. They often over-eat and become slovenly and overweight. As one captain put it, "All they do is walk around and count the bricks." This type of tedium also impacts on the firefighter's home life. The lack of purpose and contribution become part of the firefighter's daily existence, and in many instances have led to family problems and serious psychological disturbances.

The above factors are a representative sampling of identifiable sources associated with firefighter stress. However there are, as the assumption goes, many more. While firefighters experience many of the same types of potential stress-provoking situations, what determines the effects of a situation on them is their flexibility in dealing with the perceived stressor. This flexibility is most likely determined by one's own sense of adequacy, competence and self worth.

Furthermore, stress depends not so much upon what we do for a living, or what happens to us through the process of living, but rather *on the way we perceive the stressors in our life*. It is imperative for firefighters to learn how to deal effectively with their emotional tensions and how to identify and accept their physical and emotional limits.

References

1. Selye, Hans. *The Stress of Life.* New York: McGraw-Hill, 1956.

2. Selye, Hans. *Stress Without Distress.* New York: Harper & Row, 1974.

3. Selye, Hans. *STRESS: The Physiology and Pathology of Exposure to Stress.* Montreal, Canada, ACTA, Inc., 1950.

4. Selye, Hans. *"On Stress Without Distress,"* Executive Health, Vol. XI, Number 11, 1975.

SUMMARY

THE DYNAMICS OF FIREFIGHTER STRESS

Have you experienced:

Excessive weight gain or loss in a short period of time?

Frequent use of alcohol or prescribed medications?

Frequent complaints of physical distress headaches, back pain, ulcers?

More than the usual number of "accidents"?

Altered work patterns or habits?

These are but a few of the signs and symptoms of a stressed individual.

Stress is:

Presumptive; its effects cannot be seen objectively

Psychological

A specific emotional and/or bodily response

Triggered by signals in our environment or our thoughts

Ever-present in this world of many demands and pressures

More than simple nervous tension or anxieties

Neither good nor bad

The result of how we cope

THE DYNAMICS OF FIREFIGHTER STRESS

DEFINITION: Stress is the result of any demand, either internal, external or both, that causes a person mentally and physically to readjust in order to maintain a sense of balance.

STAGES OF STRESS

1. **The Alarm Stage** — a person becomes aware of a specific demand or signal requiring a response

2. **The Resistance Stage** — the mental and/or physical response to a specific demand or signal

3. **The Exhaustion and Burnout Stage** — a total inability to maintain balance because our responses (coping) are ineffective

If you aren't coping as well as you like, stop and take an inventory:

What has changed?

Who were your role models and are they still?

Is it physical, emotional, psychological?

What are your expectations and how do you perceive what is happening?

OCCUPATIONAL FACTORS THAT CAN CAUSE STRESS

The   Administration

Job   expectations   versus   reality

Color of your thinking:
　　　　　Do you see only *black and white*?

Peer pressures and expectations

CHAPTER TWO

DEALING EFFECTIVELY
WITH FIREFIGHTER STRESS

Over the years you learn to deal with the violence, just like you deal with the pain you see. People deal with it in a million different ways. You'll drink to excess. You'll take drugs. You'll go home and feel better, but it may be an unreal feeling. You'll divorce your wife or have an affair. You'll become totally antisocial. That's what I do. When I go home and I have three days off, I close the door and I don't leave. Even when we end up going out, somebody will bring it up. "Well, how's your work? What do you do? It must be so exciting. What's your worst call?" Because they don't understand, they couldn't understand.

Paramedic

Firefighters develop coping styles to quell their psychological and physical responses to stress. Over time, those coping methods may become ineffective in stemming the tide of stress and exhaustion. As shown in the dramatic example above, **one's coping methods can also contribute to stress.** This is becoming more prevalent among firefighters today.

All too often, we make the assumption that to do our best work we must generate tension and perform at peak energy levels. This is especially true concerning fire department work. In this regard, the old adage "one man's meat is another man's poison" holds true. That is to say, that what works well for one person may be dysfunctional or damaging for another; the amount of tension that one person can handle may be completely destructive mentally and physically for another individual.

As we age, our bodies do not handle sustained tension as in earlier times; things begin to break down. Each period of stress, *especially if it results from frustrating, unsuccessful struggles*, leaves irreversible chemical scars which accumulate to constitute the signs of tissue aging.[2] Just as a machine will show signs of wear and tear after prolonged use without periodic maintenance, so also does our physical system break down under chronic or prolonged stimulation. Anything can become stressful if it is strong enough, lasts too long, or is repeated too often. Similar to a broken thermostat, when the signal or "feedback" continuously reports an incorrect reading, a fire or explosion can result. In essence, *the expenditure of energy is significantly greater than the situation actually warrants!*

On the human level, many people work with "broken thermostats" and do not realize it until something goes wrong, breaks down, or they begin to develop feelings of dysphoria—the emotional state of anxiety, depression and restlessness. We begin to feel tension, life ceases to seem worthwhile, and we lose a sense of personal, occupational, and social purpose. A problem exists, often manifesting itself in irrational or maladaptive behavior, and we don't know why or how to pinpoint it. At the extreme level, the body begins to break down; stress is taking its toll!

In the emergency services environment, firemen, for the most part, show a reluctance to admit that they experience stress-related problems, or that their formerly effective methods of coping are breaking down. This is often due to two major factors common to firefighters, those being:

(1) Fear of losing the respect of fellow firefighters, and being branded as emotionally weak or inadequate.

Firefighters tend to tease or badger those among them who show any human weakness. The "grinding" starts and does not stop until the "weak firefighter" has learned to suppress his reactions and emotions by not responding to the sometimes brutal teasing of his peers. Many times a shift will start with the discussion of who will be "in the barrel" that day, or whether the "phasers" are set to *stun* or *kill*.

(2)   Firefighters compete for very few promotional spots. Thus, many firefighters believe they must be perceived by their administrators as super-heroes in the field and also in the firehouse.   It is interesting to note that within many departments, firefighter evaluations assess two primary areas of a firefighters occupational life, those being how well the firefighter functions under stressful situations and how well he gets along with fellow fighters.   Thus, the firefighter is reluctant to share his down-side emotions or shortcomings, either real or imagined, for fear that it most likely will affect his fitness report and inhibit promotability.

FIREFIGHTER STRESS AND THE TREATMENT PROCESS

Probably more than any other single factor related to treatment, none is more important than the establishment of trust and the assurance of complete confidentiality between the firefighter and the "helping" individual, be it a trained psychotherapist, a peer, someone in the Employee Assistance Program, or a close friend.

Most firefighters initially view counseling with skepticism until rapport and trust is established. They have great fear that this invasion of their privacy will result in a poor evaluation of their capabilities and possibly result in banishment to a slow fire station or at worst being put on "daylights" (working a 40-hour week, 8 A.M. to 5 P.M.). It should be further emphasized that every firefighter in distress may not relate well with just anyone in a helping environment — which is also primarily true of the general population regarding counseling. A sense of mutual and unconditional acceptance must be present to some degree before any therapeutic progress can be achieved.

When an individual is in a crisis, or experiencing an extreme stress reaction (Stage Two of the GAS) bordering on exhaustion, that person's energy is primarily expended in the attempt to maintain a sense of balance. Generally, one's level of performance, in both the personal and occupational areas of their world, is compromised. One paramedic described the feeling as simply "trying to tread water."

In dealing with manifestations of maladaptive behavior, fire administration generally recommends a change of station assignment or assignment to a daylight job. It has been my clinical experience, however, that a change of assignment is not necessary **unless** the firefighter is compromised emotionally; i.e., displaying anxiety, depression, suicidal gestures, despair on a consistent basis, or is chemically addicted to the extent that his judgment and behavior are seriously impaired. The firefighter may elect to stay in his present assignment and simply go on vacation or *tough it out*.

In many cases, just being able to emotionally express one's self and unload the "excess psychological and emotional baggage" is all that is necessary to resolve the problem for the distressed firefighter; if that is not effective, other interventions become necessary as discussed below.

LEVELS OF TREATMENT

There are various therapeutic approaches which can be utilized in developing an effective treatment plan, depending upon: the personality of the individual requiring assistance, the degree of stress or distress already present by the time he presents himself for help, and most importantly, who made the referral for assistance.

As a general rule, individuals who realize they are not coping effectively and seek counseling or psychotherapy themselves, often show a more favorable treatment outcome than do individuals who are not self-referred, such as court-referred treatment cases; these individuals are often the most resistant to outside help. Thus, for the therapeutic relationship to be most effective and productive, the individual seeking treatment must feel the need and importance in his life strongly enough to want to make a change.

There are two primary levels of treatment approaches that have been repeatedly shown to be effective in modifying an individual's level of stress as well as fostering a healthier, more effective approach to life.[3]

The first set of treatment procedures, termed "Self-Directed Approaches," provides a "cookbook" method for the resolution of one's stresses without necessarily having to be in a formal therapeutic relationship. This method may not be applicable to everyone, however. There are general principles that would also apply to the next series of treatment approaches, necessitating professional assistance, which I've termed "Community-Based Resources."

In using either Self-Directed, or Community-Based Resources, I have found it extremely helpful to have a *significant other*, close friend, or someone objective in one's corner to provide helpful feedback and validation of one's self-worth while going through the process of change. The lack of objective feedback blinds us to the realities of our own behavior. As in the analogy of the broken thermostat, we tend to hear only what we want to hear, and believe only what we want to believe, despite the pain and suffering we tend to cause ourselves and others.

SELF-DIRECTED APPROACHES FOR THE RESOLUTION OF FIREFIGHTER STRESS

Awareness Of The Problem Or Stressor Is The First Step To Resolution — The problem of dealing with stress is blocked by the reluctance or outright denial that something is wrong! Others working close to you can see it — but you won't admit it. You may feel a sense of anxiety or tension, a lack of motivation, depression, or other physical manifestations of stress, such as general fatigue, yet you still deny anything is wrong. Breaking through the denial and acknowledging that life is out of balance, is the first major step toward making the necessary life-modifying changes.

Stress Monitoring To Track "Internal Thermostat" And Increase Your Level Of Self Awareness — Stress monitoring is essential for assessing the degree of stress present in your system. Stress monitoring includes developing a keen sense of awareness of the changes in your internal state, as well as recognizing from past experience, those situations, events, and thought patterns that have a high stress-triggering potential. This includes attempting to be objective regarding the specific external stressors in your life and how these stressors were handled in the past. A helpful method for gaining a clearer picture of the problem is to pretend that a family member or close friend has been experiencing the (*your*) "problem" and has come to you for help in resolving it. How would you tell this person to deal with it? Write down your solutions for "their problem." Also, try to look at the problem area from all perspectives — almost as if it were a three-dimensional object in space. Look at it as objectively as you possibly can.

Communicate Pain With A Significant Other — It is essential that you communicate down-side thoughts and feelings, especially with those emotionally close. At the least, you must express our realization that something is amiss. Asking loved ones, family, friends, or close peers for their perception of your coping methods (behaviors) and requesting honest feedback is an important step to "opening up the closed system" which you create for ourselves. Through this process, you can begin to share your thoughts as well as your feelings. The net result is that your perception of yourself will become more crystallized, and you can begin to view yourself a bit more objectively.

Objectively Look At Your Attitude Toward The "Stressor" — **Evaluate Your Payoffs For Maintaining That Attitude** — More often than you would like to admit to yourself, you maintain certain attitudes or approaches to life such that the net payoff is feeling as though, or believing, that you are "victims" in the world. This is often a carry-over from very early childhood training. It is sometimes very surprising to discover that your early role-models acted out many of the same life patterns as you do; that you have emulated their approach to dealing with stress situations. Often, the outcome is feeling as though you're on the bottom of the rubbish heap — the result being "Poor Me!"

If you can honestly and objectively look at the payoffs of those situations that leave you constantly feeling a sense of loss or despair, then you can change your approach, that is, if you are hurting badly enough. For some, however, maintaining the role of victim relieves the responsibility for your life, and in essence, causes you to feel as though the power over your life is in someone else's hands rather than in your own. *This should be avoided at all cost!*

Lower Self-Expectations So That They Are In Line With Reality — Lowered expectations do not mean a lowered standard of living. Don't push yourself beyond what is normal and healthy (our body usually tells us what our mind doesn't want to listen to). This is especially true of firefighters who have a strong desire for promotion. Often times, firefighter's maintain an unrealistic view of their own potential or capabilities. This is often most apparent during the promotion process.

Among paramedics, for example, the feeling of omnipotence flows over into all other aspects of their lives. During emergency situations, the paramedic is in control, often having to make life and death decisions. He is sometimes even referred to as a *Paragod* by his peers as his complete desire (often out of necessity) for control is apparent. How can you expect less than perfection in a life and death situation? Being superhuman, able to respond to any emergency without losing control becomes a way of life not only at work but at home. Hence, the paramedic finds himself frustrated by an untidy, less than perfect, home.

Lowered expectations on the other hand lead to lowered levels of frustration. Frustration that continues unremitting leads directly to aggression, anger, and rage. Consequently, there is a direct correlation between our level of expectations and the stresses you experience in life. Also, lowered and more realistic expectations reduce your feeling of helplessness which is a major factor of depression.

Thus, you must learn to live more realistically with the givens of life and not push yourself mentally and physically beyond the limits of your endurance. None of you are superhuman, although sometimes you would like to believe you are and try to portray that image to others.

Examine The Personal Myths Under Which You Are Operating — Get Rid Of The Excess Psychological Baggage — Beliefs and attitudes form the most important part of your psychological makeup — they are the foundation upon which you view the world and yourself. Our self-concept is formed very early in life by those who trained us; our parents and significant others are the central figures. Your earliest social interactions also add to the formation of your belief system — how other children related to you and how you related to them, determines your socialization skills. Your sense of competence and feelings of self-worth also derive from these early life experiences.

More often than not, your self-worth, self-doubts, fears, and lack of trust, are learned as infants. We grow up without ever questioning the validity of the beliefs that you hold about ourselves and others. In essence, you are limited in life only by your belief system and the myths you create about who you are. These personal myths often go undisclosed to anyone lest they discover that possibly you don't feel as good about yourself as you would have them believe. This is the essence of excess psychological baggage. Unless you question the basis of your belief system, you will continue to carry this baggage throughout your life. I liken this faulty belief system to an old suitcase filled with garbage. One end of a rope is tied to the suitcase and the other end is tied around our neck. Once you sever the rope, you no longer have the burden of the garbage. Beliefs and fears that are irrational or inconsistent with our self-concept, weight you down and hinder your personal growth and progress in life.

An approach that may help to unburden you, begins with making out a list of your fears. Write them down. Assess how realistic they are in light of who and what you are and what you've accomplished in life. Ask yourself the question, "Are these my own fears based upon my life experiences, or are they a carry-over from childhood?" Did you learn your fears from a role-model and adopt them as your own? Finally, discuss your list with someone close to you and see how valid it is. More likely than not, you will find that much of your stress has resulted from the maintenance and defense of significant portions of this faulty belief system.

Integrate Areas Of Gray Into Your Thinking — Firefighters function within a framework of rules and regulations that define the parameters of their interactions. The world becomes black and white. Their calls become characterized as "good calls" or "bad calls," did the patient live or die? However, from the standpoint of proper mental health, there are gradations along the continuum from black to white. To the extent that you don't allow for areas of gray in your life, your perception of your world becomes distorted into bipolar evaluations. It is therefore imperative to modify bipolar thinking. Your "good-bad" evaluations directly relate to positive or negative emotional reactions without allowing for a middle ground. This might be termed the fireman or paramedic's "emotional see-saw." The emotionally healthy safety officer is one who is able to leave bipolar thinking in his locker when he takes off his turn-outs at the end of the shift.

Improve Your Attitude Toward Personal Physical Health — As previously mentioned, firefighters tend to be high-activity individuals who derive maximal stimulation from their environment. The occupation of firefighter is also highly sedentary, at times, which means the heart muscle usually doesn't get a good work-out unless the firefighter is on a regular exercise program. Exercise reduces internal pressure often felt during periods of stress. It not only tones the body, but also increases the production of endorphines in the brain — the neurotransmitter which aids in the body's healing process. Thus, the greater the commitment to a regular work-out program, the less risk of coronary artery and other stress-related diseases.

Exercise alone, however, is not the only key to good health and reduced stress levels; proper diet is the other half; and one without the other is like a car without proper fuel—you won't get very far!

Needless to say, a good physical health program precludes the use of tobacco, alcohol, and fatty cholesterol rich foods. The primary reason to discontinue fatty foods is the excess of adrenaline in the blood system when an individual is under stress. Fatty acids do not get metabolized properly, and the cholesterol is reduced to little pellet-like molecules that attach themselves and block the coronary arteries and veins. Thus, stress and cholesterol-rich foods add up to a higher risk of coronary artery disease.

Firefighters experiencing high levels of stress frequently report a lack of energy or desire to work-out. They often report that when they feel better they will begin to exercise. However, the problem becomes one like the chicken and the egg. The sooner the firefighter begins a rigorous work-out regimen, the more quickly will he begin to feel the physical relief of internal stress pressures.

COMMUNITY — BASED RESOURCES FOR THE RESOLUTION OF FIREFIGHTER STRESS

Community-based resources pertain to those sources of help or treatment available within one's community that can be used to facilitate or restore a proper and healthy balance to one's life.

If one's department has a program already established to treat firefighters and their families experiencing distress, then half the battle is won. The other (and most important) half of the battle is admitting to one's self that a problem exists. Step two relates to making the initial contact or consultation to utilize those resources, either through the departmental stress unit, Employee Assistance Program, or the services of trained and experienced professionals within your community.

The primary treatment interventions for effectively reducing firefighter stress are, but not limited to, the following:

INDIVIDUAL PSYCHOLOGICAL COUNSELING OR PSYCHOTHERAPY

This category of services pertains primarily to psychological or psychiatric intervention with a specialist trained at the level of the Master's or Doctoral degree. Initially, stress reduction counseling begins with the focus on helping the professional see the world through the eyes of the firefighter in distress. This **must** exist if counseling is to be effective. It is also through this initial process that rapport is established between counselee and counselor.

The first goal of treatment is the development of trust between client and counselor. The essence of any healthy relationship, and especially a therapeutic relationship, is trust. The establishment of trust is a necessary precondition for any therapeutic changes to occur. I have found the two primary components to the establishment of trust to be:

1) **Confidentiality of Communication** — Confidentiality is the umbrella under which therapy shields the counselee from the outside world allowing him the freedom to unlock his inner-most thoughts and feelings. In many states, however, if the counselee appears to be a danger to himself or indicates a plan to harm another, the counselor has a legal duty to warn. The client would be made aware of the therapist's legal responsibility prior to taking any action.

2) **Unconditional Acceptance of the Person Seeking Assistance** — Experience has shown that counseling sessions are more effective if conducted on at least a once per week basis, especially if the firefighter is experiencing an acute crisis or intense emotional reaction, and handled best when the firefighter is not seen during his work shift.

Although fire personnel, in general, tend to initially view therapy with skepticism, in the hands of a sensitive practitioner, many fears and doubts can be alleviated within the first few sessions. The process of uncovering problem areas and maladaptive behaviors and their remediation may then begin. In many cases, just having someone actively listen and provide objective feedback may be sufficient to resolve the problem and restore the individual to a healthy and productive state of being. Psychological counseling incorporates a number of treatment methods that are successfully used in employee assistance programs.[3] These include:

Supportive Therapy — Generally incorporates methods of providing reassurance, emotional support, psychological inoculation, such as defining for the firefighter what is presently happening to him as well as what he can or cannot expect to feel or experience as a result of his crisis. Also included are the emotional stages he will most likely go through before a resolution is reached.

Uncovering Maladaptive Defense Mechanisms — Looks at the unconscious ways in which an individual protects his ego from threat or fear. Often, one's psychological defenses may not be effective. One's own psychological defenses can work against him *causing* more pain than provide emotional or psychological protection. Learned patterns of relating may need to be replaced with more effective defenses.

Relaxation Training And Hypnosis — Can be employed to facilitate relaxation without the need for medical or chemical intervention, such as the use of tranquilizers. Using this approach, firefighters are trained to observe signs of bodily stress signals, and are taught methods for relaxing and modifying external or internal signals that have previously led to an anxiety response. Systematic desensitization is another method of reducing psychological threat or fear by replacing the signal of anxiety with a relaxation response.

Hypnotic techniques may be employed when basic relaxation methods are not strong enough to hold the firefighter's level of anxiety. Hypnosis can also be used to help the distressed firefighter uncover early life experiences that have led to maladaptive coping behaviors in the present. Additionally, these techniques can be taught to the firefighter so that he may use them on his own during periods of stress or crisis.

Assertion Training — Is a non-traditional form of expressive therapy that facilitates personal growth and behavior change through teaching one how to freely express personal beliefs, feelings, thoughts, as well as wants and needs without fear or guilt.

Through the process of self-assertion, we develop the awareness of our freedom to be, and express who we are openly and honestly, thereby fostering a sense of personal integrity and healthy self-pride. Stress can be reduced through this process because we hold nothing back, and as a result, we become more in touch with who we are.

Crisis Intervention — In cases of extreme stress reactions, crisis intervention may be used to neutralize the firefighter's response to a specific stressor which has created an extreme emotional and/or behavioral reaction. Crisis intervention may result in removing the firefighter from the work environment or may require short-term hospitalization, especially if the firefighter begins to experience a physiological breakdown, such as cardiac distress, angina, gastrointestinal or other disorders.

Alcohol And Drug Counseling And Detoxification — Many fire departments throughout the country are beginning to recognize the high incidence of alcohol and drug abuse among their employees. The detrimental effects of alcoholism are reflected in compromised job performance, and often becomes the "hidden element" leading to an early retirement!

Sometimes individual or group counseling is sufficient to alert firefighters to the warning signs and symptoms of chemical dependency. These sessions provide a forum for mutual support wherein the chemically-dependent employee can discuss his use or abuse of alcohol or other drugs without fear of retribution by his department.

If the firefighter's addiction is such that he cannot control or cease his chemical dependency on his own, the treatment of choice is detoxification, most often requiring short-term hospitalization (often a 28-day program). Supportive follow-up treatment with Antabuse, individual and family counseling, and referral to Alcoholics Anonymous (AA) are generally also significant components of these programs. Alanon and Alateen groups for members of the safety officer's family provide further support and understanding of chemical dependency and addiction. How family and friends unknowingly reinforce the addictive process is emphasized.

Marital And Family Counseling — Firefighters frequently act out their stresses within the safety of the home environment. Marital and family therapy offers all members of the family unit an opportunity to discuss openly, and without fear of retribution, problems that exist within the home.

A TEMPORARY OR PERMANENT CHANGE OF SHIFT OR ASSIGNMENT

More frequently than not, the 24-hour shift work schedule creates a disruption within the home environment, especially if the other spouse's employment conflicts with the work schedule of the firefighter. This causes major gaps in the continuity of contact with all family members. Being out of sync with the schedules of spouse and children, as well as having to work holidays and weekends, often causes additional stress and conflict in the family. The unusual shift scheduling also puts the firefighter in conflict with schedules of friends and social activities outside the fire department. Thus, the firefighter tends to associate with those on his particular shift not only while working but also during his days off. It might be argued that firefighters enjoy the company of other firefighters and therefore also associate with them during non-work or leisure time. In reality, however, it is difficult to establish and sustain a relationship outside the fire service due to the constantly changing nature of their work schedule.

THE USE OF SICK-LEAVE, VACATION OR HOLIDAY TIME, OR A LEAVE OF ABSENCE

This approach may be suggested to the employee by a stress management team or member of the firefighter's union, or by the firefighter himself, in an effort to remove him temporarily from the work environment. This may aid the firefighter in gaining a more rational perspective to his stress-related problems.

MEDICAL REFERRAL

In some cases, psychological or behavioral approaches may not be sufficient or effective in reducing the clinical symptoms of stress. If the firefighter is in an advanced or aggravated stress reaction, a psychopharmacological approach may be the treatment of choice. Tranquilizers or mood elevators may be prescribed to reduce the effects of extreme stress; especially when the effects are pronounced, such as with tremor of the extremities, chest pains, heart palpitations, excessive perspiration, and other forms of extreme autonomic nervous system activation.

References

1. Richters, Eugene. "The Knife and Gun Club." *Life Magazine*, April 1989, 52—53.

2. Selye, Hans. "On Stress and the Executive," *Executive Health*, Vol. IX, Number 4, 1978.

3. Fishkin, Gerald Loren. *Police Burnout, Signs, Symptoms and Solutions.* Los Angeles: Harcourt Brace Jovanovich, Legal and Professional Publications, Inc., 1988.

4. Ibid.

SUMMARY

DEALING EFFECTIVELY WITH FIREFIGHTER STRESS

- Recognize that a problem exists

- Break the barrier and ask for help

- Myth or reality − If I seek help, I will lose my job

- Will I be seen as "weak"?

HOW DO I BEGIN THE PROCESS OF SEEKING HELP?

- Awareness of problem/stresses/stressors

- Communicate with significant others

- Look at your attitude toward the "stressor"

- Make sure self expectations are in line with reality

- Review your beliefs and attitudes − get rid of any excess "psychological baggage"

- Integrate areas of gray into your thinking process

- Exercise and maintain a healthy diet

WHERE DOES ONE GO TO RECEIVE HELP?

- Traditional psychological counseling or psychotherapy — find a counselor you feel comfortable with. Request a temporary or permanent change of shift or assignment. Request use of sick leave, vacation time or leave of absence.

CHAPTER THREE

ANXIETY

*Man's greatest triumph
is victory over himself — his weaknesses, fears, and anxieties.*
GLF

Anxiety is as much a part of contemporary life as is food or rest. It should be no wonder that just several years ago, approximately ten million prescriptions for Valium, the anti-anxiety medication, were filled in a single year, making it the most widely prescribed drug in the world.

Frequently, firefighters attempt to "self-medicate" with the use of alcohol and other drugs in an effort to reduce their anxious feelings. That approach, however, is as destructive as the anxiety itself!

As we have seen from the examples of stress-related factors introduced in preceding chapters, and from the vivid illustration presented at the beginning of Chapter One, stress shows itself in a multitude of coping behaviors. These behaviors/reactions are expressed through physical symptoms, and differ according to the personality pattern of the individual in distress.

The emotional conditions most commonly seen in firefighters seeking psychological counseling are those of *anxiety* and *depression*. Consequently, it is important to understand these two emotional states as well as specific treatment approaches for their resolution.

AN OVERVIEW

The behavioral differences among members of the animal kingdom are as clear to us as night and day. Man is a creature of the kingdom ruled by intellect, whereas animals are governed by pure instinct.

There are critical emotional factors, as well, that separate man from other species. Where animals become alert at a particular stimulus, human beings often become anxious!

We often erroneously equate anxiety with the emotional response of fear. Anxiety, however, is quite different from fear. By definition, fear is a brief emotional state called up in response to a real danger that can be consciously identified, and defined. We know what the danger is and where it's coming from. We brace ourselves until the danger has passed or the emotional signal is turned off; then the emotional reaction of fear terminates.

Fear, psychologically, often represents a defined threat to one's physical well-being, such as entering a burning building or facing a combative patient. By contrast, anxiety most often has an unrecognizable, long-lasting effect and lingers indefinitely. Its vague feelings of mental and emotional discomfort often invade from the rear, or from all sides at once, paralyzing our senses. Mental health professionals often refer to anxiety as "psychic pain." Yet, fear and anxiety are often associated with the same physical sensations even though they are two different emotional states.

SYMPTOMS OF ANXIETY

The ways in which individuals experiencing anxiety react differ from person to person. There are, however, symptoms which are common to most individuals experiencing acute or chronic anxiety. These symptoms manifest themselves in four specific reaction patterns, those being:

1) Motor and muscular tension

2) Autonomic (automatic) nervous system hyperactivity

3) Apprehensive expectation

4) Vigilance and scanning

Motor and Muscular Tension — Common features include shaking, jitters, jumpiness, trembling, tiring easily, muscular and internal tension, inability to relax, startling easily, and the sensation of a pressure-type pain felt in the middle of the chest. Frequently, the individual experiencing an anxiety reaction is additionally fearful that his chest pain is a symptom of an impending heart attack.

Autonomic Nervous System Hyperactivity — These symptoms are: excessive perspiration, heart palpitations, clammy hands, dry mouth, dizziness, the inability to relax, and frequent urination. Gastrointestinal symptoms may be present, including: diarrhea, stomach distress, and gastroesophageal reflux (the sensation of acid burning your throat while laying down, straining or bending over). Significant problems in sexual performance may also result, as will be discussed further in this chapter.

Extreme Apprehension — Described as a persistent feeling of mental discomfort, with anxiety and worry. In most cases, thoughts center on a negative theme, such as the foreboding feeling that "something terrible is about to happen!" This anticipation may also show itself as the fear of a possible accident or of something horrible happening to a loved one.

Overly Vigilant and On Guard — "Uptight," feeling as though you're "on the edge," or "ready to scream"; impatient and irritable. Easily distracted, you may experience difficulty concentrating, develop sleep disorders or disturbances, or feel just as fatigued when you awaken as when you went to sleep, or feel worse!

ANXIETY — NORMAL VERSUS EXCESSIVE

The most important element in determining one's level of anxiety *is the way in which we perceive threat.* A normal amount of anxiety is good for us. It is useful in building our character and helping us grow, learn, and achieve as we put out our maximum effort, go the extra mile, or reach for a goal. In other words, a mild to moderate level of anxiety may be stimulating and motivating, and is a consequence of today's fast paced life style, and highly technological culture. But like *too* much of anything, excessive anxiety can be highly destructive. It can cause our reflexes to tighten, thereby immobilizing us; our normal reactions become rigid, and we develop tunnel vision regarding our perception of the stressor.

Excessive or chronic anxiety is evident when it becomes the focal point of a person's life. It generates conflict, disturbs our thinking, creates disruptive behavior patterns, and can even make us physically sick. Sustained anxiety can, and most often does, result in a breakdown of body tissue. Most frequently the weakest part of the body becomes the target of the negative effects of sustained anxiety. The result can be the development of ulcers, headaches, fatigue, heart disease, stroke, diabetes, or other debilitating diseases. Clinically, I have found that those experiencing chronic tension, frequently complain of back or gastrointestinal disorders.

Anxiety has a chemical component — the hormone *adrenaline*. When stimulated, as in an anxiety state, the adrenal gland produces adrenaline which creates the primitive "fight or flight" syndrome. During stages 1 and 2 of Selye's GAS, heart and respiratory rates increase, sweating cools the body to allow it to run from the stressor, blood vessels constrict, and the pupils become dilated so that we may clearly perceive our environment and safely deal with, or flee from, the stressor. However, in anxiety states, the stressor is usually nowhere to be found.

EXCESSIVE ANXIETY

Excessive anxiety results in a heightened sense of internal pressure and, thus, specifically affects our overall level of performance.

Anxiety also results from our psychological defense mechanisms which automatically or subconsciously protect our ego from dealing with unacceptable thoughts or impulses, such as telling the boss off, or expressing our anger or frustration, or picking a fight. We generally suppress or automatically repress these impulses, or our fantasies of acting out the antisocial behavior, due to our fear of the negative consequences of such acts.

In this regard, firefighters who maintain a very rigid mode of being and thinking often experience the effects of excessive anxiety. For many of these individuals, anxiety results from denying one's true feelings and results in a loss of self-knowledge, and emotional isolation from others. Maintaining an emotional distance prevents the firefighter from having to communicate the depths of feeling often associated with the grim realities of human suffering seen on a regular basis.

As stated earlier, anxiety in minimal amounts usually motivates a person to better performance. However, when our anxiety level becomes too great, our thoughts tend to re-run our worst case scenario; as a result of ceaselessly experiencing this anxious anticipation, our level of performance begins to decline and intervention becomes necessary.

ANXIETY AND THE COMPULSIVE DISORDERS

For some, attempts to quell the sensation of anxiety may result in the development of compulsive disorders. Examples of these behaviors are:

1) Excessive eating, frequent bingeing at the fire station

2) Workaholic-type working patterns, many times involving second occupations

3) Excessive money spending

4) Compulsive sexual behavior

5) Excessive discretionary use of power or authority

These behavior patterns relate to the excessive frustrations and boredom firefighters often experience in their daily personal and work lives. For many firefighters, compulsive behavior is also their attempt, although futile, to control their emotions externally rather than attempt to understand and deal with their anxiety and other emotions in a healthy manner. The following symptoms serve to reinforce this conclusion:

Excessive Eating/Bingeing — Eating in general serves two primary needs. The first is survival; that is, if we don't eat we die. Food is the fuel that keeps us alive and functioning. A secondary need satisfied by compulsive eating is less easily defined, and pertains more to the symbolic level of existence, i.e., food as emotional fulfillment. Individuals who often feel frustrated, lonely, bored, emotionally isolated from the world, frequently turn to food as *their* source of need satisfaction; a way of filling themselves up, especially when feeling detached, empty, and alone. Unfortunately, the satisfaction is short-lived, but the excess body tissue remains as a testimonial that *something is wrong!*

In the firehouse, meals are the highlight of the day. This is a time where firefighters can discuss issues, kid one other, complain about management, and generally let off steam.

Firefighters are conditioned to eat their meals in a hurry because of the ever impending alarm. The phrase, "Get it while it's hot," surely applies. This constant expectation or vigilance also decreases healthy digestion.

Complicating the situation is the fact that firehouses seem to have a continuous supply of sweets, including, but not limited to, ice cream and other rich food on which to binge. As one firefighter cook reported, "All you have to do is add sugar, butter, and make enough for seconds, and you're a hero."

Workaholic-Type Work Patterns — Distraction is often a handy way of not dealing with anxiety. By staying busy, we are able to satisfy our need for contact with others in socially acceptable ways. However, compulsive work patterns help us avoid confronting our anxiety, or gain further insight or knowledge as to who we are or what troubles us. Firefighters generally spend one third of their lives away from their homes and families. As a result, many cases have been reported wherein the extreme time spent at work, coupled with overtime assignments and a part-time job, had caused home and family life to deteriorate.

Excessive Money Spending — The planning and spending of money has many real and also symbolic purposes and meanings (see, for example, Chapter 1). Symbolically, money represents power and control, and spending acts as a distraction from dealing with deeper causes of anxiety or distress. As one paramedic stated, "The more tired I get, the more money I spend."

Compulsive Sexual Behavior — The sexual act has many motivations. Sex may be engaged in as a means of discharging anxiety and gaining a sense of fulfillment and pleasure. The most adult form of sexual interaction is the pleasure one shares with another as a means of enhancing a relationship. Often, when one is anxious, there may be a period of increased or heightened sexual activity as a means of discharging the internal pressures experienced. We view "performance" as compulsive sexual behavior during these periods if:

- there appears to be little or no concern for the other. The other is perceived as an "object" for the achievement of one's own sexual satisfaction or gratification.

- the gratification is used to enhance one's own sense of self-worth or self-esteem.

- the sexual behavior is a substitute for some other need that is not being satisfied in a healthy, appropriate way.

The situation is worsened when we are not aware of the basic needs we are attempting to satisfy through our sexual interactions. Thus, while we may temporarily distract ourselves through the discharge of tension, we get no closer to an understanding of what is prompting our anxiety or stress.

The downside of anxiety and compulsive sexual performance is that too much anxiety may create a state in which the individual becomes sexually dysfunctional. In the male, the symptoms show themselves as:

- a significantly reduced or absent sexual drive

- the inability to maintain an erection

- premature ejaculation

- a combination of all of these factors

In the female, either loss of sexual drive, or inability to achieve lubrication, causing pain, may result from excessive anxiety.

After a major incident or fire, many firefighters

experience an overwhelming sexual need; an all-consuming desire for release of tension. This desire for release is not unhealthy, but rather represents in a nonverbal way, the firefighters need for recognition, nurturing, and support.

Excessive Discretionary Use Of Power — This form of tension release may serve to assist the firefighter in discharging frustration and anxiety, but often reinforces his belief that he must be in control. The effect of this over-generalization serves to skew the working firefighter's perceptions of his role in society, and also encourages the belief that there is no basic right, that authority is precarious or capricious. Heavy-handed paramedics and fire officers are found in many fire departments.

HOW TO DEAL WITH ANXIETY

In the treatment of anxiety, there is not one primary approach that works with all individuals all of the time. Certainly, each of the treatment approaches discussed in Chapter Two would be applicable in aiding fire personnel experiencing either acute or chronic anxiety. Therefore, to avoid unnecessary repetition, treatment approaches previously cited will not be rediscussed here.

In general, professional experience has shown that regular exercise and proper nutrition would be at the top of the list of approaches to the resolution of anxiety. Lowering or eliminating the consumption of processed sugar has been shown to reduce the effects of anxiety and depression in both children and adults. The use of alcohol to self-medicate should be discontinued as should stimulants such as tobacco and caffeine.

Friends and loved ones can be of great help when one is feeling extremely anxious. Talking about one's problem reduces the "inner pressure" experienced from attempting to cope with anxiety, and helps to lessen the feelings of isolation and alienation we experience when caught in the grip of anxiety. Clinical experience has shown the following approaches to be most effective in the treatment of anxiety:

Self-Disclosure, Communication, And Catharsis — Central to overcoming anxiety is the ability to release pent-up emotion which blocks healthy functioning and limits our ability to explore new solutions. When we are in the grip of an anxiety reaction, our ability to perform healthy problem-solving becomes blocked. Our emotional signal reads RED — the alarm is on, and we are in pain. During an acute anxiety reaction, exploring alternatives or developing insight into our "problem" is about as effective as rearranging deck chairs on the Titanic! During these stressful periods, one needs a trusting friend, time-out, and a degree of self-disclosure. Self-disclosure is accomplished through the process of communication, the safety valve of our intellectual and emotional systems; the means by which we can begin to articulate our innermost wants, needs, fears, and other hidden thoughts. Thoughts that are hidden from the rest of the world and, most importantly, from ourselves, are the ones that often create the most pain for us. The most healthy environment is one in which there is unconditional acceptance, thereby allowing us to open up and face the truth of who we are and what our pain is all about.

Take Time-Out To Gain A Perspective — Like battle fatigue, being on the front-line too long wears us down. In a similar way, the effects of anxiety — adrenal pressure and psychic pain also — tear us down. Taking a spontaneous vacation, going off for a weekend, or getting away from the familiarity of our own environment helps to free ourselves from the internal pressure and pain. Also helpful in coping with the effects of anxiety is extending one's self emotionally to the needs of another. This takes the focus off of our own internal stress. The act of compassion, which may be considered a form of distraction, has certainly proven to be effective in restoring emotional balance to one's life and also benefits others in the process.

Cognitive Restructuring — This approach involves the reframing of situations in our mind in order to render them ineffective in producing anxiety, thereby reducing our stress level. The restructuring of thoughts may be directed at modifying the meaning of the stimulus or perceived stressor, as well as our sense of adequacy in coping with the stressor. This powerful form of therapy utilizes rational thought processes as a first line of defense against anxiety. Emotional reactivity or anxiety is called into play before rational thought and generates the most pain. Thoughts take only milliseconds to pass through our brain. Yet what is triggered by negative thinking may last from minutes to hours, and sometimes days or longer. Thoughts directed at some event in the future are the primary source of anticipatory anxiety. We can liken anticipatory anxiety to the experience of stage fright. "What will happen to me?," "How well will I perform?" or "Will I be accepted?" are common themes in our thinking, and the outcome is usually negative! It is that instantaneous charge of negativity in our thinking that stimulates the adrenal gland to cause a jolt of anxiety which sets our autonomic nervous system racing; our heart begins to pound, breathing becomes rapid, and pulse rapidly accelerates. The automatic thoughts which triggered anxiety responses in the past can be brought to the level of conscious awareness and modified so that we can attain a more rational way of thinking and coping. In addition, the stressed firefighter is trained to interpose an interval of time, one to several seconds, between a stimulus (either a thought or perceived demand) and his usual response to it. The goal of this type of treatment is to reduce or eliminate our automatic emotional reactions to our mental content and to replace it with a less negative, less self-defeating pattern of thinking. To develop a more positive, self-accepting set of attitudes serves to reinforce a healthy, more adequate approach to life and a significant reduction in stress. This method of therapy is also highly effective in the treatment of depression.

TENSION REDUCTION STRATEGIES

As stated previously, anxiety causes or stimulates hormonal changes within the body in the form of increased production of adrenaline, which in turn creates sensations of discomfort and internal pressure. Other physiological and neurological changes also take place during acute or chronic anxiety that result in heightened arousal, vigilance, and activation of the autonomic nervous system.

Tension reduction methods are aimed at lowering one's state of arousal in an effort to restore a sense of balance and also to facilitate improved performance and a sense of well-being. These strategies are aggressive approaches employed to combat the negative effects of anxiety. Tension reduction methods fall into four primary categories:

1) Exercise   3) Hypnotic Procedures

2) Relaxation Methods   4) Medical Intervention

1.   **EXERCISE** — As many can attest, after a rigorous workout, we experience a heightened sense of well-being and internal peacefulness.   When we are in a heightened state of alarm, we often feel as though we are going to explode.   Regular rigorous exercise allows for the physical discharge of tension.   Additionally, (during at least a forty-five minute workout), brain endorphines are released, stimulating the nervous system in such a way that physical pain is relieved and a sense of well-being is experienced.   Endorphines are the brain's neurochemical equivalent of morphine.

Exercise has also been found to have a profound effect in the treatment of compulsive disorders;   primarily compulsive eating, more commonly referred to as binge eating.   Experience has shown that firefighters under stress, especially if anxiety and frustration are present, often binge eat in an effort to   "fill themselves up."   This provides a feeling of immediate gratification as a result of their work effort.   This is especially true after a large fire or following an intense rescue effort.   The firefighter also feels that he has earned a reward.

When weight loss becomes a goal of a stress reduction plan or program, it must be emphasized that neither diet nor exercise alone is sufficient to cause healthy weight loss.   Both diet and exercise must be used in conjunction with one another for a program to be effective.   This is primarily due to the body's weight "set-point" concept.   Individuals attempting to lose weight through diet alone often complain that at a certain stage their weight loss reaches a plateau, beyond which bulk simply does not come off;   each person's metabolism slows down to a certain level in order to compensate for a reduction in caloric intake.   This level is called the "set-point" or maintenance level of the body.   If this were not the case, individuals dieting, either intentionally or not, would starve much sooner than is usually the case. The primary way of tricking the body's set-point is through the process of regular exercise. Through exercise, we speed up metabolism, give the heart a healthy work out, and increase the probability of tilting us off our weight plateau toward a more desirable appearance and a greater sense of self-control and mastery over our being.

2. RELAXATION METHODS — These approaches counter the physical effects of anxiety through methods that are "antagonistic" to the stimulation of the adrenal response. The primary idea underscoring these methods is that an individual cannot be anxious and relaxed at the same time. That is, anxiety and relaxation are antagonistic to one another. Therefore, through training individuals in the use of relaxation methods, we can teach them to substitute a relaxation response to stimuli that would generate an anxiety response. These methods are easy to learn and often provide immediate relief from tension. These approaches fall into four categories:

- Progressive Relaxation

- Breathing Exercises

- Systematic Desensitization

- Meditation

Progressive Relaxation — Jacobson's Progressive Relaxation Method, named after its founder Edmund Jacobson, M.D.[1] Underlying this method, the belief that relaxation must be learned and that nervous disturbance is correlated with mental disturbance. By teaching individuals to progressively tighten and relax all parts of the body in a systematic way while lying down and breathing in synchrony with the release of muscle tightening, one can achieve a state of tension reduction and deep body relaxation while remaining awake and alert.

Breathing Exercises — Breathing exercises compensate for the shallow breathing that occurs when one is experiencing symptoms of anxiety. Shallow breathing does not allow for the healthy exchange of oxygen and carbon dioxide. Consequently, the type of rapid, shallow breathing that frequently occurs during acute anxiety often results in hyperventilation or the depletion of carbon dioxide from our system. As employed by such diverse professionals as singers and athletes, breathing exercises require training in diaphragmatic breathing in an evenly timed rate. This approach should be practiced daily, such that when we become aware of anxiety and consequent automatic shallow stress-breathing, we can adjust our level of breathing so that a healthy respiratory balance is restored. In order to receive maximum benefit from this approach, one should be laying on one's back and should relax the muscles in both the chest and abdominal area while breathing in and out.

Meditation — There are many forms of meditation, and I do not sanction one over another lest we lose sight of the meaning of the process itself. Meditation is a form of centering one's entire mental effort on a quiet, peaceful thought. Through this process, our energies are focused on a deep level of thought, free of value judgment, or even awareness of self. Through the process of meditation, which can be accomplished in almost any setting and even during one's work shift, a sense of internal quiet and peace can be obtained with almost no effort. Meditation has been shown to be of great value, especially during periods of anxiety and crisis.

Systematic Desensitization — Often used in the treatment of specific fears, this approach is also very effective in the treatment of anxiety. This method requires the subject to develop a hierarchy of fear-producing situations, and through the use of visual imagery, substitutes a relaxation response for the anxiety we would usually experience. This hierarchy often begins with situations that have a low potential for causing us anxiety, and increases in increments to situations that would previously immobilize us with panic. The concept behind this approach is that we cannot be anxious *and* relaxed at the same time.

3. HYPNOTIC PROCEDURES — Sometimes referred to as autosuggestion or hypersuggestibility, hypnosis, when facilitated by an experienced practitioner, can be very effective in modifying unhealthy thought and behavior patterns. As differentiated from sleep, individuals under hypnosis are aware of their surroundings and are in control of their own reactions. The therapist is merely the facilitator of the hypnotic experience which is akin to a very deep state of relaxation and heightened suggestibility. As stated previously, anxiety specifically affects performance levels. Hypnosis can be employed to reduce the sensation of anxiety through the neutralization of stimuli that triggers the anxiety response. Additionally, hypnosis can be employed with visual imagery to facilitate a positive self-concept through the development of more relaxed, assertive social skills. Hypnosis is also used to uncover and modify unhealthy psychological defenses and to produce a more open, less fearful pattern of thought and behavior. Contrary to popular belief, individuals under hypnosis will not say or do anything that is intolerable or antagonistic to their own sense of morality. This allays a frequent fear of those who have not had direct experience with this powerful treatment approach.

4. MEDICAL INTERVENTION — In the event that non-medical efforts prove ineffective in resolving the anxiety reaction, medical attention should be sought in order to rule out organic factors that may be causing this emotional state.

In cases of *extreme* anxiety, tranquilizers may be prescribed as an adjunct to verbal counseling. This stabilizes the patient and enables therapy to be effective. As is often the case, when anxiety levels are very high, attention and concentration spans are short, thereby limiting the beneficial effects of counseling and psychotherapy. Individuals in a state of high activation should have a complete physical examination in order to provide a comprehensive evaluation of their mental and physical status.

A combination of several of the treatment approaches mentioned above can be used in reducing or eliminating the effects of extreme anxiety. It should also be kept in mind, however, that anxiety, in *moderate* levels, is as much a part of contemporary life as are any of the other states of being one might experience in day-to-day living. A healthy attitude is one in which we do not allow ourselves to succumb to self-pity, but rather, rise above our experience and do something constructive to effect a positive change in our lives and the lives of those we touch.

References

1. Jacobson, Edmund, M.D. *You Must Relax.* New York: McGraw Hill, 1978.

SUMMARY

SYMPTOMS OF ANXIETY

- Muscle tension

- Shakiness, jitters — motor tension

- Hyperactivity

- Apprehensive expectation — "something is about to happen to me"

- Uptight, on edge, difficulty sleeping

IF ANXIETY CONTINUES UNCHECKED, COMPULSIVE DISORDERS CAN APPEAR

- Excessive eating

- Workaholic type work patterns

- Excessive money spending

- Compulsive sexual behavior

- Excessive use of force

HOW TO DEAL WITH ANXIETY

- Regular exercise

- Proper diet

- Share emotionally with significant others

- Take time out for "yourself" — treat yourself to a weekend way

- Help others — the act of compassion helps restore balance

- Cognitive restructuring — develop a positive attitude

- Breathing exercises

- Relaxation methods and exercises

- Meditation

- Hypnosis

- Medical intervention

CHAPTER FOUR

DEPRESSION

The experience of depression contains a particular irony. Having started out to help others, we somehow become wounded ourselves.
GLF

W hat happens when the plans, hopes, and dreams we hold for our lives become thwarted; when our expectations for ourselves, no matter how unrealistic, lead us constantly to a sense of letdown, frustration, despair, anger or aggression? For some, the result is the emotional reaction of depression. Depression is not the result of a single element or experience, it is the painful, emotional outcome of an interaction of factors. These factors include: our genetic and biological make-up, our early life experiences, the type of role models we emulate, our unique way of perceiving the world and processing information, and how we handle frustration.

The focus of this chapter is to provide an understanding of the factors related to the emotional state of depression. Additionally, this chapter identifies characteristics which differentiate firefighters who have worked through depression, from those who have not been as fortunate.

From my clinical observations, it is significant to note that, in most cases, individuals experiencing a primary depression show symptoms similar to those patients experiencing exhaustion-burnout (stage 3 of the GAS). However, we must not confuse depression with burnout. Although it is a fact that symptoms of depression are present in burnout, as will be shown in Chapter 6, the burnout syndrome is far more complex. It is far easier and less costly to treat depression than allowing it to continue into a burnout condition. *If depression continues unremitted, it will result in occupational burnout.*

We have all experienced small doses of depression at some time in our lives, and possibly larger doses during the active phase of a life crisis. Hopefully, we recovered with few scars, and gained some new insight about life and who we are. For some, however, the combination of life's calamities, a poor self-image, and a perceived inability to effect change in the world, becomes too much to bear. The result is often a breakdown of psychological defenses, leading into the downward mental and emotional spiral of despair, ultimately leading to depression, from which the road back is often painful and difficult.

THE SYMPTOMS OF DEPRESSION

There are a number of symptoms usually present and generally shared by those experiencing a major depression. Depressed individuals are often not aware of the emotional changes taking place within them. Yet their families, friends and co-workers, are able to see quite clearly the all-encompassing effects of the depression.

The following symptoms are generally seen in most cases of primary depression, with some variation based upon the individual's personality characteristics:

Dysphoric Mood — The symptom most generally associated with depression is the all-pervasive sense of doom and gloom, that *sinking* experience that is so often equated with a feeling of "internal death." As this mood takes hold, the pain becomes so great that there is a resultant loss of interest in previously gratifying pursuits, such as hobbies, sports activities, and other pastimes.

Social Withdrawal — Loss of pleasure and meaning in life has a profound effect on one's family and one's social sphere. It is as if the depressed individual crawls into a cocoon in order to protect himself from the outside world. Yet in reality, the individual's internal process, not the outside world, is primarily responsible for his depression and the resulting sense of loss and despair.

Anxiety, Fear, and a Heightened Concern Regarding Physical Ailments — These symptoms form an important aspect of the clinical picture of depression. Anxiety, which is very often the result of changes in brain chemistry, may take the form of psychomotor agitation, tremor, tenseness, irritability, and incapacity to experience a sense of comfort and peacefulness. Individuals in depression generate thoughts of a foreboding nature. Anticipation of the unknown also adds to the state of anxiety, compounding the symptoms of depression.

Psychomotor Retardation And Significantly Decreased Energy Levels — The neurochemical theory of depression postulates that the neurotransmitters, norepinephrine (the brain's equivalent of adrenaline) and serotonin (which is similar in action to adrenaline), are absorbed by the brain in an accelerated fashion when one is in a state of depression. This process is equivalent to an out-of-tune carburetor that uses too much gas, and takes in too little oxygen, so that the engine lacks the energy to do its job effectively and efficiently.

Appetite Changes — This symptom is manifested as either a loss of interest in food or compulsive binge eating. In the latter case, most patients state that they eat, not because they are hungry, but rather from a deep sense of frustration or anger, the causes of which they do not understand. In either case, the person experiencing depression will often exhibit a marked change in body weight. If there is a significant increase in weight, it may be due in part to a decrease in metabolism. It should be emphasized that among the firefighter population, a form of "chemical depression" resulting from alcohol abuse or improper diet, is often a factor in the case of the depressed individual.

Sleep Disturbance — Insomnia, dreams filled with themes of self-condemnation and guilt, and an inability to maintain a sound state of sleep, are common characteristics of sleep disturbances occurring during depression. Firefighters experiencing a major depression, frequently complain about waking up feeling fearful and shaky. If they do manage to overcome their restlessness and fall asleep again, upon awakening they often feel as tired or even more so than when they first went to sleep.

Thoughts of Low Self-Esteem and Self-Worth — Depressed individuals' thought patterns are dominated by repetitive ideas. These vary from feelings of inadequacy, to unrealistic, negative evaluations of one's self-worth or one's worth to others. This sense of worthlessness, helplessness, and hopelessness, often representing a distortion of reality, serves to reinforce their negative belief systems. The depressed individual looks for signs confirming his own negative sense of self-worth. This is validated unconsciously by the self-fulfilling prophesy (we usually get what we expect from the world).

We fail to realize that subconsciously we help to bring about many of the negative occurrences in our lives. Thoughts of low self-worth can be brought on by physical problems or a disability which forces the firefighter to be removed from the work environment. Disability brings about an emotional sense of loss which often triggers depression. This is especially common with firefighters that are no longer able to perform or compete with peers and that have no avocation, hobbies, interests, or friends outside of the fire department. For many individuals, the role of firefighter has been their primary identity and the focus of their lives. Thus, the loss of professional status frequently leaves one bereft of personal identity, creating a sense of despair that may be overwhelming.

Distortions of Thinking and Faulty Information Processing – Such as **a)** overpersonalization, i.e., relating everything in the outside world to one's self, even if no logical connection truly exists, **b)** overgeneralization – always on alert, waiting for the alarm, ever vigilant for a crisis or calamity, **c)** an increase in bipolar thinking (good or bad evaluations), and **d)** magnifying or minimalizing events out of proportion to the demands of the situation. As depression worsens, this can also lead to a profound disorder of thinking, an inability to mentally focus or engage in effective problem solving, and losses in short-term memory.

Suicidal Ideation, Thoughts of Death, or a Suicidal Gesture – Thoughts of suicide and death among the depressed symbolically represent a desperate need to escape the emotional pain and turmoil of depression, and find a way out of their feelings of guilt, despair, loss of mastery in one's environment, and ultimately, a loss of hope, meaning, and purpose in life. Suicidal gestures represent the ultimate need to get beyond the pain of attempting to cope and survive in the world. The method one chooses may either be very obvious, or may be disguised in the form of an "accident." Among suicidal firefighters, the inability to mentally focus, coupled with a poor reaction time, may lead to: a lack of vigilance, unnecessary risk-taking without adequate protection (such as not wearing breathing apparatus), intentional recklessness, especially during a code 3 response, lack of precaution in a dangerous setting, not being safety conscious, and other possible situations which could ultimately result in a fatal accident or serious injury.

THEMES AND ISSUES COMMON AMONG DEPRESSED FIREFIGHTERS

When closely examined, interviews of firefighter experiencing depression each showed common factors that formed central themes in their psychological profile. The following themes were observed in firefighters who have been treated for depression:

- Lack of assertiveness and a basic feeling of inequality within an aggressive paramilitary organization oriented around macho-competitiveness

- Aging firefighters who see themselves as being on the downward tail of productiveness to society, especially those who have "retired" to slow fire stations

- A sense of helplessness to effect a change in society

- Depression as a result of the effects of alcohol abuse and improper diet

- Constant harassment and heckling by members of the department

- Anger that is suppressed or repressed

- Marital, family, or personal problems that may seem insurmountable and interfere with the demands of the job and expectations for role performance

- Futility in attempting to please others

- Emotional sensitivity that is continuously suppressed or repressed in order to meet the demands of the job

- Depression as a result of unresolved trauma due to an especially shocking incident

- Depression related to the internal conflict between emotional dependence (on a job or a person) and a need for independence

- Constant exposure to the lowest and most degrading aspects of life; hopeless frustration as one begins to see that things don't change, or as one safety officer has said, "Same shit, different day!"

- Anger and bitterness toward life resulting in a skewed perception of reality

- Depression resulting from ongoing internal departmental conflicts and problems

- The growing realization that one's personality and needs are mismatched to the demands of the job

- Depression in relation to an extreme sense of pride that blocks one from disclosing or discharging deep-level emotions

THE COURSE OF DEPRESSION

The symptoms of depression generally result in one of three outcomes, those being:

1. Resolve with time, support, and psychological treatment.

2. Remain at approximately the same level for a long period of time. Some individuals exist in a state of depression for years before the emotional wear and tear brings them to a lower level of emotional functioning.

3. Worsen to the point where the individual becomes personally and occupationally dysfunctional.

One would hope that adequate insight or prompting from peers, friends, or significant others would help to bring about a resolution as indicated in outcome #1 above. As is so frequently seen in the professional consulting room, outcome #3 is the inescapable result of the constant, ongoing internal pressures and external demands that reduce one's coping process to the point of exhaustion. The effects of stress are cumulative, and a lowered threshold for tolerating frustration is usually present when one is in a depressed state. For the firefighter experiencing the effects of severe depression, it is inevitable that he be taken off active duty as his ability to perform in a safe manner, and to provide public service consistent with social expectation, is compromised.

THE TREATMENT OF DEPRESSION

It is often far easier to identify the existence of a problem than it is to resolve it. Nothing could be more true regarding the treatment of depression. The two cases of depression presented here exemplify the different courses of action and outcomes individuals may experience in working through the painful experience of depression.

As it progresses, depression becomes much more difficult to resolve; therefore, it is very important that it be detected and treated in the early phases. However, case histories have shown that most individuals experiencing depression will not seek outside assistance or treatment until the emotional pain is either unbearable, or they become totally dysfunctional. This is particularly a problem with males, in that only a small percent of men experiencing extreme distress, as compared to females experiencing similar symptoms, show a willingness to make the initial consultation for help. *Therefore, acknowledging the existence of the depression is the first step toward treatment.*

There is no one course of action or primary treatment approach agreed upon to deal with the symptoms of depression. However, I have developed an effective system of procedures which have resulted in positive outcomes for treating depressed individuals.

It must be emphasized, however, that unlike other emotional or adjustment reactions or disorders, if the depression does not resolve itself within a two-week period from onset of symptoms, the individual will most likely require psychological or medical intervention.

Since depression is a biopsychosocial disorder, it

touches all aspects of our psychological, social and physical life. Therefore, a combination of treatment modes becomes necessary.

On the individual level, approaches related to the self-help treatment of depression include:

Exercise — Either begin an exercise program, or increase your current program, so that you are exercising at least three times per week. This may include a formal workout regimen at a gym, jogging if your physical status and weather conditions permit, bicycling, or some other type of defined exercise program that you enjoy. The exercise that a firefighter receives during the performance of his duties is *not* the same as a healthy workout program. Vigorous workout has been shown to increase the production of the neurotransmitters norepinephrine and serotonin discussed previously. The restoration of the supply of these two naturally-occurring brain chemicals acts as a natural antidepressant and serves to facilitate mood elevation without the need for chemical intervention.

Monitor Your Diet — Modify your diet to compensate for caloric intake levels and metabolic changes within your body. Take heed not to binge eat, or the opposite, to starve yourself, during a depressive episode. Frequent cravings for unhealthy foods may lead to increased levels of depression. One should completely discontinue the intake of processed sugar in any form during a time of depression or crisis, as sugar acts as a chemical pick-me-up on the one hand, and creates an increased feeling of dysphoria or depression on the other. Stimulants such as caffeine and nicotine should be avoided for the same reasons. If one's diet is not modified during a depression, it then becomes very difficult to distinguish the psychological triggers or emotional factors of depression from the effects of chemical depression which are often self-induced and diet-related.

Discontinue The Use Of Alcohol And Other Central Nervous System Depressants — The use of alcohol should be totally discontinued at the first symptoms of depression. Alcohol, acting as a central nervous system depressant, is sufficient enough to create the chemical symptoms of depression in healthy, functioning individuals. It stands to reason that its use or abuse during depression only heightens the symptoms of depression and reinforces one's poor coping mechanisms and chemical dependency needs. The discontinuance of chemical depressants includes tranquilizers, antihistamines, cough suppressants with codeine and certain prescribed medications which may have a chemically depressing effect on the central nervous system. These *chemical depressants* mask the non-organic, emotional factors of depression. If you are uncertain regarding the particular effects or side effects of a medication you are taking, check with your physician. In many cases, alternative medications may be prescribed that do not have a narcotizing effect on one's physical and mental behavior.

Change Of Assignment — A temporary or permanent reassignment may be requested as a means of removing the individual from environmental stressors that may be triggering or exacerbating a depressive reaction. Cumulative stress overload resulting in a depression is often treated by changing one's occupational environment.

Request Time Off Or A Leave Of Absence — In extreme cases of depression or emotional exhaustion, it is imperative that the firefighter avoids the psychonoxious work environment. He will need time and space in order to disengage his thinking from the role stressors associated with his occupation. When depression begins to take hold, the importance of getting away from the work environment cannot be overemphasized. During this period, the individual must be encouraged to rest and relax. Healthy pastimes might include: developing a new hobby or re-exploring old ones, changing one's daily routine and approach to life, learning to develop spontaneity, and learning that during time off, one does not have to do anything. Firefighters frequently believe they have to be doing something much of the time. Learning to relax leads to a healthier life. Often, doing nothing is actually doing something! It is allowing our emotional and physical systems to repair themselves through the process of rest.

Since extreme depression is a manifestation of stage three of the GAS (Exhaustion), relaxation becomes of prime importance and is often a new learning experience for the firefighter who equates productivity with self-worth. One must overcome the sense of guilt that is experienced when one is not working. Also, during this time, a re-evaluation of one's meaning and purpose in life should be undertaken. As so often happens with depression, there is a loss of meaning to one's life which leaves an emotional void that must be filled.

Individual Counseling And Psychotherapy

External interventions are necessary elements of a comprehensive treatment plan for depression. The experience of depression carries along with it a unique set of circumstances and conditions; hence, approaches aimed at resolving depression experienced by firefighters should incorporate the following:

Catharsis — the discharge of cumulative, suppressed or repressed emotion that is often at the core of depression. Once the individual has vented his emotions, he will feel a sense of relief from the pressure of depression. His mood will be elevated and he will have a better outlook on life.

Because their symptoms have been lessened, oftentimes firefighters discontinue therapy at this point, believing their problems are resolved. Ongoing treatment during this period is essential. Also important at this time is supportive counselling, ego-strengthening therapy, and the development of healthier defense mechanisms. It is during this early stage that patients must learn that suicidal thoughts are a normal part of depression and learn not to fear their presence since they will go away as the depression lifts.

Assertion Training — Since depression often has at its roots a sense of helplessness, blocked anger and fear of confrontation, assertion training provides the opportunity to respond to old stressors with new and healthier thoughts and behaviors. The benefit is a healthier self-image, one that is more congruent with a positive outlook on life. This is frequently an extremely important aspect in the treatment of depression. Many community colleges offer classes and programs in assertion training.

Cognitive Therapy — This form of treatment, which is relatively nonthreatening, challenges the belief system of the depressed individual in an effort to restructure faulty thoughts invariably present in the mind of the depressed individual. The "poor me" irrational thought processes are modified so that the "bucket is half full rather than half empty." Of absolute importance is learning to see one's world from a different perspective — redefining one's self and life conditions allow for the production of alternatives and new thinking. Consequently, by helping to refrain one's irrational and self-defeating thoughts, we are able to derive a sense of power and control over our own thought processes.

Supportive Family Therapy — Wives, husbands, girlfriends, boyfriends and peers, are often the first to make a consultation appointment regarding their depressed loved one or friend. They are also first to express their concern for the safety and welfare of the individual. Family therapy brings the depressed individual's social-emotional network into the treatment scheme, and provides the opportunity for the sharing of information and allows loved ones to discharge their own feelings and thoughts in a safe, accepting, non-judgmental environment. It further allows the counselor to observe interactions between family members which may be adding to the build-up of stress and subsequent depression.

Determine Presence Or Extent Of Substance Abuse And Necessary Treatment — If one is unable to discontinue the use of alcohol and/or other substances, appropriate treatment measures must be undertaken and will be discussed at length in Chapter 7.

Medical Consultation And Evaluation — Depending upon the extent of the symptoms of depression, a medical evaluation to determine the possible necessity of antidepressant medication or other medical and pharmacological needs may be in order. In extreme cases, the individual may require short-term hospitalization. This provides a stable environment in which to monitor high-risk suicidal individuals. Medical evaluation is also part of a comprehensive work-up should a permanent leave of absence or stress retirement become necessary, or Worker's

Compensation claim filed.

Disability Retirement — Sometimes the unique combination of factors, both internal and external, interact in such a way that the only viable alternative for the safety and well-being of the firefighter is retirement. The grooves of depression may become worn so deeply over time as to preclude the possibility of returning to work. The cumulative effects of stress resulting in and from depression may also be seen as a form of "combat fatigue." Placing a depressed firefighter back in service is equivalent to putting a rifle back in the hands of a mentally, physically, and emotionally worn-out soldier, and then ordering him back to the front lines to fight! The results would be, and have been, disastrous.

Thus, while depression may be a significant factor leading to burnout, and also present in a burnout condition, it is by no means the entire process. Burnout, as we shall see, has multiple roots and symptoms.

SUMMARY

SYMPTOMS OF DEPRESSION

- Feeling of gloom and doom
- Loss of pleasure and meaning — social withdrawal
- Decreased energy levels
- Anxiety and fear of creating actual physical ailments
- Loss of interest in food or compulsive eating
- Occurrences of sleep disturbances
- Thoughts of low self-esteem and self-worth
- Distorted thinking
- Thoughts of death, suicide, or escape fantasies

PERSONAL TREATMENT OF DEPRESSION

Identify and accept the signs of depression in its early stage

- Begin or increase you exercise program
- Monitor your diet
- Discontinue the use of alcohol and other depressants
- Request a change of assignment
- Request time off or a leave of absence — learn to relax — it's OK to do nothing

INDIVIDUAL COUNSELING AND PSYCHOTHERAPY SHOULD ADDRESS

- Catharsis — discharge cumulative, or suppressed emotions

- Assertion training

- Cognitive therapy — process of changing thoughts and attitudes — learning to see life from a different perspective

- Supportive family therapy

- Extent of substance abuse and required treatment

- Medical evaluation

- Disability retirement

CHAPTER FIVE

THE DYNAMICS OF CRISIS

In every age "the good old days" were a myth. No one ever thought they were good at the time. For every age has consisted of crises that seemed intolerable to the people who lived through them.

Brooks   Atkinson

Firefighters deal with human tragedy and crisis on a regular basis. Yet, they disregard or deny the effects on their emotional system. Every life and death experience leaves its emotional imprint on us. Often misunderstood is the fact that there is a cumulative effect (or emotional build-up) of dealing with crises, especially without the benefit of "emotional decompression," or distance from the demands of crisis situations.

A crisis does not always lead to burnout. Crises are energy-depleting, and if the emotional reaction to a crisis is not resolved effectively, burnout can occur. Our response, triggered by a crisis or traumatic event, is determined by our perception of the event. That is, how we see it determines our reaction to it. The frequency of dealing with crises, and our emotional responses to them, must also be clearly understood.

Typically, the emotional experience of crisis causes one to feel tense and confused. You feel as though you are in a personal emergency situation. Psychologically, the future becomes uncertain and you are unable to understand the reason(s) for these feelings, and even more threatening, you do not know how to stop the reaction!

Each of us has our own unique style of dealing with a crisis. The most typical reactions are: feelings of loneliness, despair, self-absorption and self-pity; a belief that no one can know how isolated and in pain we feel. We begin to believe that our reaction to the crisis is abnormal. Rather than face what we believe to be potential ridicule, we withdraw instead, isolating ourselves from others. In doing so, we block the possibility of gaining honest, healthy feedback, and comfort from those who, having experienced a crisis, can fully understand and appreciate at a deep emotional level what we are going through.

CRISIS DEFINED

A crisis is an acute stress situation which is perceived as one's own sense of self. The individual cannot clearly see what is happening to him, nor what is likely to happen. Distortions of perception and truth are not unusual or uncommon. The most typical responses are manifested in: depression, confusion, anxiety, a foreboding panic, a feeling of impending loss, shock, and sadness.

In dealing with either a loved one, or a peer in a crisis, or possibly yourself, it is important to know the following phases of a crisis:

- Feelings of helplessness which increase tension — "What can I do to relieve this horrible feeling?"

- Mental confusion compounded by loss of memory — difficulty in problem solving

- Repression or suppression of emotions, especially anxiety or physical symptoms, accompanied by a loss of reality testing or the ability to adequately differentiate between one's emotional state and the external world

- Denial is often the defense mechanism that operates during loss of reality testing

- Inability to predict tomorrow, the crucial factor of a crisis

- Lack of understanding as to why an event has come about or what the event is going to do; "What will happen to me next?"

- The loss of psychological and emotional equilibrium followed by attempted resolution and heightened mobilization of resources

- Often, sexual disinterest follows the initial shock of a crisis. This is seen as a way of relieving anger, anxiety, and post-crisis tension. Additionally, I have found that many firefighters use sex to reinforce their sense of self-worth or self-esteem, which has been deflated by the emotional whirlwind of the crisis.

A crisis tends to bring out the best in some people and the worst in others. Major life traumas such as divorce, or death of a loved one, can precipitate a crisis, just as can the loss of a job or being told that you require surgery. In any case, crisis is as much a part of life as are the non-stressful, happier times of our lives. As with most situations, the important factor is how you deal with the crisis.

CRISIS AND TRAUMA

A crisis may result from many causes. A sampling of

stressors that may trigger a crisis reaction are:

- A major disaster, such as an airplane crash with many fatalities — especially children

- The loss of one's home; or an act of God, such as a devastating earthquake

- An acute traumatic injury resulting in a chronic physical disability

- Being sued as a result of a work-related situation including wrongful death wherein a patient dies, or negligence in controlling a fire incident

A crisis is not the same as anxiety, depression, or trauma. Rather, there are components of each of these emotional states within the crisis syndrome itself.

POST-TRAUMATIC STRESS DISORDER AND CRISIS

This disorder, first diagnosed among combat veterans and victims of war, has also been identified in children who have witnessed violence. Sufferers of Post-Traumatic Stress Disorder (PTSD) appear to be caught up in a state of emergency, displaying exaggerated biological responses to even minor stresses.

Symptoms of PTSD typically result from exposure to a single traumatic event, such as a natural disaster, plane crash, flood, or other natural or man-created catastrophe. Symptoms of PTSD have been variously referred to as "battle fatigue" or "Viet Nam Syndrome."

Symptoms of PTSD include re-experiencing the traumatic event while awake and asleep, increased irritability, and a numbing and distancing of one's self from the outside world both physically and emotionally. Anxiety and depression are most notably present. A loss of previously rewarding hobbies and interests generally follow exposure to a traumatic event.

Symptoms may be present at the time the trauma is experienced, or may appear six months to years afterward.

Sleep disturbance, hyper-alertness, and increased startle response, are commonly experienced. Patients report loss of emotional and sexual intimacy, as well as emotional explosiveness, irritability, and sometimes unpredictable aggressive behavior.[1]

To cope with their psychological and emotional reactions, suffers of PTSD sometimes resort to substance abuse in an attempt to numb their memory of the trauma.

The treatment of PTSD may incorporate all of the interventions described at the end of this chapter.

Post-traumatic Stress Disorder and burnout are not synonymous disorders. In PTSD, the cause is related to a specific and unusual life event that is acute and identifiable. Burnout exhaustion, as we shall see, results from the cumulative effects of attempting to cope with stressors that are often chronic and undefinable for the individual.

Individuals living through a major life crisis do not see the world as being orderly and predictable. Rather, they experience a sense of chaos and imbalance in their lives which shakes the very foundation of their existence.

The following narrative poignantly details a 16-year veteran firefighter's experience with a devastating trauma and it's personal aftermath:

On February 27, 1988, I was working an overtime on a paramedic engine in the south end of our city. On that night at approximately 3:00 a.m., we were rung out to a reported structure fire. From all the years that I've worked here, you learn to tell by the inflection in the dispatcher's voice if it is something or if it's a nothing call. We got the feeling as we were awakened that this was really something. After leaving the station looking north we could see flames. The fire had already vented the roof, and was coming out the front door probably 10 or 12 feet.

As we were walking towards the house with the roof ladder we were notified by the battalion chief that there were 2 children trapped in the house and Ted Johnson and I were to go in, search and rescue. We entered through a front bedroom window which was heavily charged with smoke. We had breathing apparatus on but because of the excitement, the fact that there were kids, we neglected for our own sake to take a charged line with us. When we got in and started to make our search we found a crib and a bed and between the crib and the bed we found a very small child, she turned out to be the youngest of the Martino family. She was 2 years old.

It's very traumatic to find a limp, pulseless kid, but we passed her out the window. Ted and I then continued our search. It was so smokey that you really couldn't see your hand in front of your face, you just had to go by touch and feel. We found another bedroom door and opened it, went inside and Ted went to the right, I went to the left and that's where I found

Melinda Loper. I took my air mask off after taking a deep breath of air, put the mask over the young girl's face, and made a bee-line for the window. Again, passed her out, and followed her out. I told my captain that Ted was going to be right behind me. As I got outside we learned that there were up to 4 more children still in the house, so I told Ted that I would start resuscitation efforts on the first two kids and for him to go ahead and continue the search.

I was doing CPR on the kids side by side, alternating breaths from one to another and in between times shouting out instructions on what equipment I needed, getting quick paddle checks between both kids, getting EKG's on them, and placing advanced air ways. While I'm doing this, every time I turn around they're passing me out another kid in full arrest. There was a total of six on the curb with me. At this time, we had extra ambulances coming in to help transport, I had shouted out that I needed some more help to the battalion chief and he had another squad respond. About the time they got there we had somehow mustered up enough people that CPR was in progress on all the kids. They were being disbursed to all the different hospitals. I stayed, probably as a matter of the attachment to the child, Melinda, the six-year-old, that I had rescued, and went with her to the hospital. I wanted that kid to live.

It wasn't until hours later, at daylight, that we started sorting out what had happened when the Lopez family came to pick up their girls and looked and saw the house burnt down. We didn't even know what hospitals they were at; we didn't even have names on these kids yet.

The children were from two different families. There were some from the Martino family and some from the Loper family. The Lopers, this was the first time they had ever left their kids anywhere. They had four kids there, four of the six. They had left them there, for the first time, the first time they ever walked away and left their kids anywhere and came back the next morning and the house was burnt down, and all we could say was their kids were at different hospitals. They had to go all around the county searching them out and identifying either their kids, deceased, or the Martino kids, deceased. Mr. and Mrs. Martino were sedated and hospitalized because they were so out of it. So you went from the initial shock and tragedy of seeing this house on fire, the screaming, the yelling, the panic, everything going on, during the rescue and the resuscitation attempts and then the next morning the pieces of the personal tragedies of these families starting to come together.

They told me a long time ago when I started this that I should never be more involved with patients and just to be concerned for their basic care. That's not the kind of person I am. I've always felt that being a paramedic was my calling in life. So during this period of time I came to know the Martino family, the uncles, the brothers, cousins, whatever, and the Loper family, because it was again Melinda that I rescued probably got me a little closer to them. One day I asked them to get together, both families, with their priest and to meet us at a local mom and pop type cafe in town. Mrs. Loper pulled out a letter that Melinda had wrote Friday at school, her last English assignment, concerning what she wanted in life. I couldn't remember it right now word for word but the gist of it was she knew that her family was poor, that there was lots of love and she loved all her brothers and sisters and she hoped someday to be famous and be on television. She had been, for two weeks.

She died four days after the fire. She lasted the longest, everybody was either dead on arrival at the hospital or died within hours after being brought in. I mean, two were resuscitated, Melinda being one, and she lasted four days. I wasn't there the day she died; I learned about it on the radio.

The day after this meeting, during the night, I woke up out of a sound sleep crying after having a nightmare where I returned to the scene of the fire and the house was not burned down but was bright sparkling white. Melinda was laying on the bed, not on the floor. The bed was made perfect, and she was bright, shiny clean and cheerful, happy and sat in my lap and wanted me to explain to her the things that she was going to miss in life. She asked me questions about what it was like to have children, to be a mother, and how she wanted a puppy. She wanted a house so she could have a puppy of her own and this kind of stuff. There were things that I learned from talking to her mother. In all my experiences as a fireman and paramedic and after seeing many bad things this is the first time this had ever happened to me and I felt like "I had cracked" after always trying to be macho and think that you can handle stuff. This was a shock to me to think that I couldn't. Shortly thereafter the city sent me to a psychiatrist where I explained the story to him. He told me that it was a very textbook case that I wasn't crazy and I went back to duty that day and pretty much have lived through it.

I still have flashbacks of the experience. The only thing that I've really been thinking about off and on is the anniversary date, which is just a few weeks away and the fact that I promised myself that I would contact the family then and that I would go and put flowers on all the graves of the kids.

The city had a psychiatrist come in and counsel everybody who had been on duty that night. From the time of the fire to this meeting, most of us, all of us had joked through, not really joked through it, but tried to get through it, dealt with it the way we had dealt through everything else. With levity, humor, just saying the feeling that we're macho and it doesn't bother us. And while you're doing all that external stuff what was happening inside? Most of us were pretty screwed up if you really want to know. We had a meeting and most of us were feeling like, what do we want to talk to a shrink for, we're not crazy, that's a waste of time. He got in there and started us talking, we shared a lot of things, feelings, a few quivering lips, a few tears running down the cheeks. Off and on we spoke about what we felt. They asked me what bothered me the most about it. It was the futility of everything we did and that nothing worked. I mean guys gave, not 100%, not 110%, but 150%. You couldn't have asked for more people doing more things and everybody putting out everything you can. Two guys doing CPR on four kids. Everybody went above and beyond. And then to do all that and have six kids all perish was more than any of us could handle. If one would have lived, it would have been enough and anything after that would have been gravy. But for all of them to die was just a nightmare. One captain that we have, he's kind of one of the guys we kick around because this guy is all work, no play, no humor, never smiles, Mr. Rock, and he talked about it as a supervisor trying to protect his men, trying to give them the direction to do what they needed to do to get something done. He broke down and wept like a baby. That was all we could take, the shrink was crying too.

The public has the attitude, the feeling we're all that's between these people out there and their own demise and we're strong enough to handle that and we can go out and mechanically do our job the best we can and go back to the station and wait for the bell to ring again. But we're not that tough. They don't make people that tough. If they made you that tough, you wouldn't be in this line of work.

I couldn't sleep after the fire. I stayed up for 48 hours, I didn't sleep for the whole next two days. It was like I had to constantly be doing something. I went home I hugged my kids, loved them, cried, we cried, and then I got in the car and came back to town and worked for two days. This job's pretty heavy sometimes!

||||||||||||||||||||||||||||||||||||||||||||||||||||||||||||||||||||||||||||||||||||||||||||||||||||||||||||||||||||||||||||||||

OVERCOMING A CRISIS

In the general case, the passage of time alone is sufficient to restore adaptive psychological and emotional functioning after a crisis. However, frequently a professional therapist may be consulted in an effort to obtain objective, supportive assistance of a short-term intervening nature, especially if what is needed is the learning of new, more effective coping techniques.

Psychotherapists who treat counselees caught in the grip of a crisis should never use a "shotgun" type of therapeutic approach with these individuals. Rather, therapists must make a precise assessment as to the specific stage of stress (i.e., alarm, resistance, or exhaustion) the counselee is in, and use intervention techniques appropriate to their mental and emotional status.

For example, in the case of divorce or the breakup of a relationship, the individual may feel totally alone in the world. Emotional support by others should be sought-out in order to bridge the gap and reduce the sense of isolation, aloneness, and need for validation felt by a person in a state of crisis. Family and friends are often the first line of support.

A major catastrophe evokes a feeling of overwhelming anxiety and tension because our previously effective, learned means of coping, are no longer useful in extinguishing the overwhelming sense of emergency experienced during a crisis. Things happen so quickly that one has neither the time nor the mental and emotional wherewithal to develop new behaviors to cope with the stressor. Thus, stress inoculation methods, including role-playing and other techniques aimed at helping crisis victims learn to deal with ambiguous situations are appropriate. This can also be accomplished by the fire department at the level of basic recruit academy training and fire officer training programs.

In the event of a major disaster, such as the loss of one's home through fire, earthquake, or other acts of nature, it is often useful to help the individual perceive the situation in a different light. Through cognitive restructuring, a method of modifying one's thoughts, perceptions, and emotions related to a situation, an individual can be helped to reframe his loss in such a way that he is not immobilized with grief and despair. Fostering a sense of thankfulness to be alive and hope to rebuild can often help facilitate a more positive attitude about one's acute life situation.

Stress inoculation through training in problem-solving methods can offer individuals the ability to "invent" a multitude of options and approaches that can be utilized in working through a specific life crisis. As an example, a firefighter develops a ruptured spinal disk. Rather than withdraw into depression and despair, he can request a second opinion, determine all possible or available treatment approaches including specific physical therapy, and attempt to deal with his options in a rational, non-emotional way, rather than framing his situation in terms of the loss, the end of his career or the end of his active physical and social life.

During a crisis, the need for total and complete withdrawal must be countered with the understanding that reaching out to others to share our sense of grief, loss, and despair — bridging the gap between ourselves and others — is a major step to becoming more healthy.

In order to heal, we must also be able to derive a sense of meaning and purpose from our suffering. To understand the why of our grief can help provide the how of our survival.

Finding within ourselves the courage to continue, and compassion for the needs of others, provide a helping hand during times of our own grief. A case in point is the growth and development of the organization Mothers Against Drunk Drivers (M.A.D.D.), which grew out of the grief of a Texas woman whose daughter was struck down and fatally injured by a drunk driver. Rather than withdraw into her own sense of loss and despair, self-pity and aloneness, she reached out to others, and found that there were hundreds of other families who shared the same grief. This act of compassion, of turning outward and focusing one's attention to the needs of others, of helping others through a tragedy or trauma, becomes a way of self-healing.

Essential to the process of healing is allowing kindness and forgiveness within ourselves, freeing ourselves of guilt and self-condemnation for things beyond our power to control or change. In fact, the only thing we truly have control over and can change in life is our own attitudes. Dr. Victor Frankl,[2] the world renowned psychiatrist and founder of *Logo* (meaning) *Therapy*, and foremost writer on the Nazi concentration camps, stated that when stripped bare of all one's worldly goods, possessions, and family; standing, in the middle of a concentration camp room naked before the commandant of the camp, the only thing he had control over was his attitude. He had a choice as to how he would let the situation affect his judgment, attitude, and will to survive. Through his own ordeal, he discovered that meaning is essential for survival. Those in the camps who lost any meaning in life also lost the will to survive and subsequently died. Others who were prodded by Dr. Frankl to find even the smallest meaning in their lives, survived.

There is no question that a *crisis* calls up all of our resources. The more creative and able we are to distance ourselves emotionally from the crisis stressor, the more effective we will be in handling life's fateful downside.

References

1. American Psychiatric Association. *Diagnostic and Statistical Manual of Mental Disorders* (Third Edition — Revised). Washington, D. C.: American Psychiatric Association, 1987.

2. Frankl, Viktor E. *Man's Search For Meaning.* New York: Simon and Schuster, 1962.

SUMMARY

CRISIS

Crisis is an acute stress situation that is perceived by the individual as a threat to the self and includes:

- Feeling of helplessness

- Mental confusion

- Repression of emotions

- Lack of understanding as to why this is happening

- Inability to predict tomorrow

WHAT CREATES A CRISIS?

- Major life traumas such as divorce or death of a loved one

- Loss of job

- Major disaster such as airplane crash, loss of home

- Acute traumatic injury

TREATMENT OF CRISIS

- Seek emotional support from others

- Consult a professional therapist or psychotherapist

- Develop a positive attitude

- Provide support and help to others

PTSD AND TRAUMA

- Created by natural disaster

- Catastrophe — natural or manmade

- Loss of home

- Death of someone close

TREATMENT OF PTSD

- Talking about the trauma

- Share with other trauma victims

- Help others

- Time heals all wounds

CHAPTER SIX

FIREFIGHTER BURNOUT

Only the stress of frustration, of lack of purpose, can spoil the satisfaction of performance.

Hans Selye

Previous chapters explored the individual signs, symptoms, and conditions associated with the Burnout Syndrome. Chapter Six studies the firefighter burnout phenomenon, what it is, and what it represents to the individual, his department, his family, and peers.

BURNOUT — A DEFINITION

The classification of *burnout* is not found in a psychological or psychiatric diagnostic manual. Burnout is not a clinical diagnosis. Burnout is experienced internally, as a state of exhaustion, and reflected outwardly, through behaviors employed to maintain a state of balance. Burnout is the interaction of:

- pre-existing personality factors

- life experiences

- psychological needs and expectations

- environmental conditions

The factors stated above result in the inability to function effectively in any aspect of one's life. Burnout affects all aspects of being, psychological, emotional, social, physical, or occupational.

WHY BURNOUT?

Members of the firefighting profession, due in large part to shared personality characteristics, values, interests and needs, define themselves by what they do occupationally. Many individuals who enter firefighting as a career derive maximum gratification and reinforcement from external or environmental stimuli, more so than from pursuits of intellectual insight or self-awareness. In keeping with these personality needs, their self-concept becomes identified with their occupational and social roles, and encompasses a significant portion of their lives. Thus, they often come to feel as though they are one with their occupation.

Those who over-identify with their work begin to overpersonalize it during burnout. Events on the job affect them after the shift is over.

Yet, firefighters are more than their job; they are individuals who experience anger, violence, despair, and the agony and sorrow in which we all live.

When a firefighter has an unclear perception of who he is, and has no balance of recreational and healthy social interaction, he becomes lost in the world around him. He becomes one with the misery he sees in his day-to-day work. Ongoing departmental hassles, and difficulties between co-workers and supervisors, significantly compound the problem. Each day becomes an instant replay of the day before! It is no wonder that feelings of *cynicism, disillusion, demoralization, and despair* are generally felt and verbalized by those in a state of burnout.

Thus, the firefighter's perception of life becomes limited by his last experience, and his inability to separate himself as an individual from his firefighter role. As the internal pressures mount, a sense of dissatisfaction with life begins to increase as well.

Life never runs smoothly, there's a daily buildup of energy which **must** be discharged. When this energy is not discharged effectively, when we begin to feel the pressures of life both internally and externally, when old coping mechanisms no longer hold back the waves of anxiety, fear, despair, and meaninglessness of life, when there is no relief from the ongoing pressures of life and there's nowhere to hide, we have entered the domain of burnout!

In burnout we become one with our judgments of life, which, in this condition, are mostly negative. We also begin to see ourselves as "victims," without power and control to effect a change in our lives. Feelings of helplessness, despair, depression, and isolation are pervasive in our subconscious both while awake as well as during our attempts to sleep. A hollow, empty feeling is felt physically and is related to the deep sense of depression which is an integral part of the burnout experience. The profound sense of helplessness and hopelessness to change one's life situation most assuredly adds to the creation of depression experienced in burnout.

As burnout progresses, "meaning" and "purpose" in life become shallow and empty concepts that provide no residual spark to ignite the will to continue to cope with life's demands. In severe cases of burnout, one's will to live sometimes becomes so severely compromised that death is often seen as the only option out of this state of mental and emotional misery. In essence, burnout forces us to distance ourselves from the source of stress and the demands upon us which, in burnout, seem overwhelming.

During the burnout process, we experience the need for withdrawal or escape from our environment. In some cases, this results in passive withdrawal, such as getting fired, injured, or "accidently" killed. However, a less final outcome of burnout, from the occupational standpoint, is the granting, by departments and agencies, often unwillingly, of early stress retirements. The following case history vividly illustrates the process and outcome of burnout.

A CASE OF BURNOUT

Terry Ashford is a tall, well-built, 41-year-old male Caucasian who, for the past ten years of his life, was employed as a firefighter/paramedic. Terry Ashford burned out. This case highlights many of the clinical aspects of burnout that have been observed among individuals who no longer are able to effectively perform their work as firefighters.

SELF REPORT ||||||||||||||||||||||||||||||||||||||||||||||||||||||||||||||||||||||||||||||||||||||||

Above all else, I like to be liked. Because of this need I go overboard to please those around me, especially people in authority. Face-to-face confrontations are distasteful to me. In many instances, I will avoid confrontations or situations where others are in conflict. I'll turn away so not to become involved.

My need to be liked has led to problems in my career as well as personal life.

On occasion I have overreacted to this need to be liked by demonstrating what might be described as a selfish attitude toward those who would normally try to please me. I would also try to express an attitude of "I don't care." This expression of contrary feelings creates a lot stress for me.

I hate to do the same thing day after day. My desire for change has had an enormous effect on my life. It seems that I must be stimulated continuously or I become quite uncomfortable. I also become agitated if I don't have anything planned for the day, in fact, I almost become panicked. I think that my job as a paramedic also attests to this need for order and stimulation.

I rapidly develop enthusiasm for new ideas, and I lose interest just as fast if the new thought becomes monotonous.

Another trademark of my personality which attests to my high behavior control and self-esteem needs is that I like to make fast decisions. Having to delay a decision makes me angry because I feel that I already have all the information needed to proceed. Sometimes I feel I am overloaded with too much information.

I often become obsessed with resolving problems. This tendency may also be the reason for my desire to make rapid decisions. The need for problem resolution is stressful for me, but I currently attempt to control my obsessive thoughts. I do this by diverting my attention to something else and will keep my mind too busy to dwell on a situation.

Pressure develops for me from my desire to be the best in my field. I feel this pressure most in my professional and my scholastic endeavors.

In dealing with stress, I also attempt to resist dwelling on situations that I can not change. I try to remember that I cannot control every situation in my life.

When I'm in an overload situation, I must realize that this is stressful for me. I must then stop and think about, rather than react to, the situation at hand.

BACKGROUND

Terry, the second oldest of four siblings, grew up in very comfortable surroundings. Terry's mother is a housewife and his father is a very successful engineer who is self-employed. Upon graduation from high school, Terry enlisted in the United States Marine Corps, obtaining the rank of Sergeant E-5. He served a tour of duty in South Vietnam during the Tet Offensive in 1968. He received the Naval Commendation, Presidential Unit Citation, and Combat Action Ribbon.

He has been married for sixteen years. His wife is a schoolteacher. They have three children, a son age twelve, and two daughters, ages eight and five. Terry is very attached and devoted to his family.

Upon separation from the Marine Corps, Terry attended a local community college, receiving his Associate in Arts degree. Because of his intense desire to serve his community, he applied for and passed the written and physical examinations for firefighter.

He began his firefighter career working at a large mountain-resort fire department. He worked there for approximately three years. Feeling the desire to work in a metropolitan area, he and his family moved approximately 150 miles to a community of 68,000, where he was employed as a firefighter/paramedic.

After two years, he hired on to a larger department where he maintained employment as a firefighter/ paramedic for the last six years of his career as a firefighter.

At the time he joined his present employer in 1983, Terry was already experiencing anxiety and depression as a result of his employment as a paramedic with his previous employer. His symptoms increased when he was assigned to paramedic work in 1984. Shortly after, Terry began having intermittent gastrointestinal problems, insomnia, anxiety and depression. About that time, he experienced bouts of alcohol abuse, especially when anxiety symptoms first appeared. However, after several years of self-medicating with alcohol, he abstained due to his physical problems as well as the negative effect it had on his family life, especially in light of his father's own history of alcoholism.

He indicated that he found the work of a firefighter less stressful than his duties as a paramedic. His symptoms temporarily abated. However, in November 1984, he was assigned full time to his department's paramedic program. Although an experienced paramedic, he felt the work was too stressful and preferred remaining in the role of firefighter without paramedic responsibilities.

In 1984, Terry experienced a flare up of his gastrointestinal distress and insomnia. He experienced a gradual buildup of anxiety and depression during 1985. In

1986, he sought consultation with a physician through his prepaid health program and received Tagamet for his gastrointestinal symptoms. He was reluctant to transfer out of the paramedic program as he was hoping that his medication, along with some additional time to adjust, would help him cope with his situation. In 1987, Terry was preparing for the paramedic recertification examination. He was also studying for the promotional exam to become fire engineer. On his own, Terry began to see a psychologist for his symptoms.

In the weeks prior to his first psychiatric evaluation, his symptoms had exacerbated. On June 15, 1988, Terry was seen for his first psychiatric examination. Excerpts from his first exam indicated that during the early 1980's, the patient suffered from increased anxiety. In 1982, he felt agitated and depressed, and had suicidal ideation. He attributed this to the stressors of his job. Terry continued to be intermittently depressed and anxious, also experiencing insomnia and gastrointestinal distress. At the time of his psychiatric examination, Terry was on the list to be promoted to engineer. He felt he needed to leave the paramedic program.

On April 4, 1988, the patient had a busy day at work. He had 19 calls and felt pressured. After a day off, Terry returned to work and was criticized by his supervisor regarding his paperwork. Later that evening the patient received four more calls at work and felt overwhelmed. He told his battalion chief that he wanted out of the paramedic program. He broke down and cried, and was placed on disability. Seven days later he returned to work. Terry was reassigned to a slower station as a firefighter. He complained of feeling anxious and apprehensive. He was frightened and concerned about the people he treated as a paramedic. He was worried about children dying or being hurt. Mr Ashford stated that he had difficulty handling life and death situations. He felt responsible for people and ruminated over the incidents.

Terry was diagnosed as suffering a generalized anxiety disorder with depression and psychological factors affecting his physical condition, manifested by his gastrointestinal distress. It was medically felt that his treatment was required for an occupationally-related disorder, and eight additional sessions of psychotherapy were recommended to help him adjust to leaving the paramedic program. By not returning to his position as a paramedic, Terry would be considered permanent and stationary, as far as his workers' compensation disability claim.

PSYCHOLOGICAL REPORT

The patient appeared to be suffering from acute job burnout resulting from prolonged stress due to his service as a paramedic and firefighter. At the time of the psychological report, it was stated that the patient had been in treatment for six months. Terry suffered from stress, depression, fear, nervousness, insomnia, gastric problems, disturbing dreams, trouble concentrating, and generalized anxiety. The psychologist recommended that the patient not return to work on an active status as either a fireman or paramedic.

After five months of treatment, Terry continued working as a firefighter until September 1988. The treating psychologist felt that it was in his patient's best interest not to return to either paramedic or firefighter work as the jobs were too anxiety-producing for him.

Terry's emotional condition fluctuated over the ensuing months. He was on the promotion list to become an engineer, and was still motivated to remain with the fire department. However, with the passage of time, he experienced a gradual deterioration of his emotional condition marked by increased feelings of anxiety and depression. He had several good days, but there were also many bad days. He felt that his stomach distress was worsening. He would take an occasional Valium to alleviate his anxiety as well as his muscle spasms, which he was experiencing frequently.

Terry had difficulty coping with calls that required him to utilize his abilities as an Emergency Medical Technician, especially during the last three months of his employment. He had one call just before his disability leave wherein a 15-year-old boy had been shot in the head. The patient described the victim as lying in a pool of clotted blood. He was able to provide adequate care for the boy, but began brooding about this incident.

Concurrent with increasing thoughts about the victim, Terry experienced an increase in his anxiety level. The patient had obsessive thoughts about his 12-year-old son who could have had the same thing happen to him. Terry related that approximately a week after he responded to the call for the 15-year old boy, he "collapsed" in bed. He was severely depressed with suicidal ideation.

The patient does not believe that he can be involved in any work which has him dealing with injured people. Terry feels that he has been so sensitized to firefighting and trauma that he can not return to work for his employer or any other fire department. Terry claims that he has lost confidence in himself.

PSYCHOLOGICAL EVALUATION SUMMARY ||||||||||||||||||||||||||||||||||||||||||||||||||

Psychological testing indicated that, in general, the patient anxiously seeks reassurance from others and is essentially vulnerable to fears of separation from those who provide support.

Although seen at times to be submissive and cooperative, he has become increasingly unpredictable, irrational, and pessimistic. Repeatedly struggling to express attitudes contrary to inner feelings, he often portrays conflicting emotions simultaneously toward others, most notable those of love, rage, and guilt. Also notable are confusions over his goals and identity, his highly variable energy levels, easy fatigability, and an irregular-wake cycle.

Particularly sensitive to pressure and demands, he frequently vacillates among being socially agreeable, sullen, passively aggressive and contrite. He has learned to anticipate disappointment by constantly questioning and doubting the genuine interest and support shown by others.

In the recent past he has begun to exhibit helplessness and clinging behaviors, as well as suspicion, anxiety and depression. The inability to regulate his emotional controls, the feeling of being misunderstood, and the erratic moodiness all contribute to innumerable wrangles and conflicts with others and to persistent tension, restlessness, and depression.

He fears facing his feelings of unworthiness and because he senses that his coping defenses are weak, withdrawal from society appears to be his only option.

PHYSICAL   COMPLAINTS

From a psychiatric standpoint, Terry presented the following complaints:

- Stomach distress, worse under any pressure.

- Heart palpitations which may occur under stress or without any obvious stress.

- Feelings of anxiety and apprehension. Terry sleeps from 5 to 9 hours a night. His appetite is good. He continues to have dreams of some of his traumatic calls. His dreams are disturbing and may awake him out of a sound sleep. He worries about his children being hurt. His tolerance for frustration has diminished. He has problems concentrating and attending.

SUMMARY

Despite ongoing supportive psychotherapy, and a reassignment to a less stressful position at the firehouse, Terry was never free of emotional symptomatology.

On one of his last calls, he was confronted with a young boy who had sustained a gunshot wound to his head. Terry became overwhelmed with anxiety and was placed on disability status by his treating psychologist. Terry began to feel slightly better since being away from the work environment. However, he continued to be apprehensive which he attributed not only to the sequels of his employment, but also to the uncertainty of his future.

Terry is a very pleasant individual who suffered long-standing occupational problems. He had prior suicidal ideation. He had problems dealing with life and death situations.

Terry is a compulsive individual who feels overly responsible for people. His insecurities and anxieties had pervaded all aspects of his employment situation. It would be medically improbable that he could return to work as a firefighter.

Terry also feared that co-workers who had known him as a firefighter and paramedic would look down on him and make him the focus of jokes. This had occurred in the past when people had humorously referred to him as "crazy" for seeing a psychologist.

In summary, Terry became so sensitized to his employment with the fire department that it was in the best interest of all parties that he be medically retired.

Terry stated that he will seek employment as a teacher or become self-employed as a handyman where he is responsible to himself.

REMARKS ||||||||||||||||||||||||||||||||||||||||||||||||||||||||||||||||||||||||||||||||||||||||||||||||||||||||||||||||||||

For Terry Ashford, the need to avoid emotionally stressful work situations can be attributed to his employment as a paramedic. What remains for him as a result of his career as a paramedic, are very deep valleys of depression, anxiety and despair. In March of 1989, Terry Ashford was formally retired from his occupation as firefighter/paramedic.

PRIMARY SIGNS OF BURNOUT

The following signs and symptoms of burnout among members of the firefighting community indicate a remarkable similarity. The symptoms of burnout manifest themselves in the primary areas of a person's life, those being:

1) Psychological   3) Work

2) Physical   4) Family

The primary features and symptoms related to the burnout syndrome have been discussed at length in the preceding chapters, therefore only a reference will be made in this section in an effort to avoid redundancy, and as such, only the symptoms pertaining to exhaustion will be highlighted.

PSYCHOLOGICAL AND EMOTIONAL SIGNS OF FIREFIGHTER BURNOUT

- Most, if not all, of the clinical signs and symptoms of anxiety or depression as presented in Chapters 3 and 4 are present during the acute phase of burnout

- Psychological exhaustion including mental fatigue and significant loss of motivation

- Significantly reduced levels of tolerance for frustration and ambiguity

- A profound sense of helplessness and hopelessness regarding one's life situation

- A feeling of doom and anxious anticipation of the future

- A widening gap in one's black and white evaluations; becoming more judgmental

- A heightened sense of cynicism and distrust of others

- An increase in alcohol and/or other substance abuses

- Thoughts related to death and suicide; often followed by a feeling of profound sadness, grief and occasional tearful outbursts. For some, anger and rage may be displayed as an emotional defense against deeply felt feelings of sadness and the need to escape feelings of turmoil and pain

- Inability to perceive or generate alternative solutions in order to bring about a positive change in one's life

- Fear of impulsively acting out the overload of feelings bottled-up inside

- Irritability, aloofness, and social withdrawal

- Feelings of social and emotional distance from one's peers as well as feelings of social alienation

- Profound loss of a sense of orderliness and predictability in life coupled with a resultant loss of a sense of personal control and mastery over one's life

- Occasionally, a sense of disbelief that the burnout phenomenon is occurring, even as psychological and emotional defenses continue to deteriorate. These individuals often report, "I can't believe this is happening to me!"

- Despair; previously rewarding activities become lost to "just getting through each day"

- Disillusionment regarding one's life, career and the world in general

- A loss of spiritual values

PHYSICAL SIGNS OF FIREFIGHTER BURNOUT

- Exhaustion; loss of energy, drive or motivation; feeling of constant lethargy. Burnout victims often complain of being tired all of the time

- Physical illness, traumatic injury or bodily complaints. The symptoms vary widely but may include mitral valve prolapse, gastrointestinal disorders, tension headaches, chronic neck or back pain, hearing impairment, high blood pressure and possibly more severe cardiac problems, and numerous other physical disorders

- Muscular tension

- The physiological symptoms related to depression and anxiety

- Sleeping difficulties such as insomnia. The sense of exhaustion is ever present, especially when awakening from the attempt to rest or sleep

- Muscular tension and a feeling of internal pressure

Frequently, pressure behind the sternum is felt in the acute phase of burnout.

OCCUPATIONAL/VOCATIONAL SIGNS OF FIREFIGHTER BURNOUT

- Increase in the number of emotional contacts with the public; feeling loaded with frustration, anger, despair, and fear

- Increased absenteeism, use of sick leave, vacation and holiday time, leaves of absence and Injury Disability off time

- Low level of morale, including feelings of isolation and aloneness at work. The firefighter won't share these feelings due to fear of peer reactions

- Significant loss of, or reduction in, efficiency and work productivity; perceived by others as significantly reduced job performance; may be accompanied by administrative reprimands

- Increased number of hangovers while at work

- Over-personalizing with the job and with one's own work efforts which, in burnout, are perceived as negative. Everything becomes a "personal matter"

FAMILY-RELATED SIGNS OF FIREFIGHTER BURNOUT

- A feeling of physical exhaustion when coming home from work

- A feeling of emotional "distance" from spouse and children

- In the case of burned out male firefighters, the wives most often take over the primary responsibilities of running the home and maintaining the continuity of family support and discipline. For the burned out female firefighter, the husband often reluctantly assumes all responsibility for home and family, thereby creating an imbalance within the family system.

- Refusing to participate in family or social events

- A reluctance to initiate any activities that would draw the family unit together

- Verbal and, sometimes, physical abuse of family as a means of venting internal pressure

- A complete lack of interest or desire for sexual sharing. If sex does occur, it may be very selfishly motivated.

- A need to place responsibility for this condition on outside factors and circumstances. The family often becomes the brunt of tensions, frustrations, and conflicts. Separation and divorce may result.

THE TREATMENT OF BURNOUT

Just as the experience of burnout is a multi-dimensional process with many features and causes, so too is its treatment. Since burnout is primarily a mental phenomenon often manifested with physical symptoms, it stands to reason that bringing about a resolution requires intervention in the areas affected, specifically the psychological, emotional, family, and physical aspects of one's life.

Vocational rehabilitation is also a necessary component of a complete treatment program. For in the majority of cases of occupational burnout early retirement is inevitable. Thus, problems related to the loss of occupation, the need to restore mental, emotional, and physical well being, and the need to re-establish a sense of personal identity and self-worth, signal that there are many areas of life to be addressed in the process of healing those suffering burnout.

PSYCHOLOGICAL AND EMOTIONAL TREATMENT OF BURNOUT

Since the primary symptoms of burnout are manifested as either anxiety or major depression, or a combination of both, the treatment plans and the specific interventions outlined in each of the preceding chapters should be followed.

By the time the burned out firefighter is presented for treatment, he is either on a leave of absence, or should be. Consequently, time off from the job is mandatory in most cases. However, depending upon the degree of denial present regarding his condition, getting the firefighter to accept his situation and the potential outcomes may be difficult. Generally, however, the physical symptoms related to the state of exhaustion and its manifestations are significant enough to alert the individual to the fact that he is in extreme stress and medical attention is needed.

Supportive counseling and individual psychotherapy, as well as family counseling, are a central focus in the treatment of burnout cases. The sense of personal isolation must be bridged to allow others to enter into the emotional life of the firefighter in burnout. This is achieved through psychological counseling and therapy.

Peer group support is also necessary, especially if there are members in a support group who have successfully weathered the effects of burnout.

Issues related to self-worth, self-image, and one's value to others become a major topic of psychological treatment. In this regard, from the therapist's standpoint, what one hears and sees during the counseling situation with burned out firefighters is far different from how the firefighter portrays himself to the world. It is the deep emotional sharing that individuals in burnout need to learn to express, which in time helps reduce their distrust and distance from what they perceive to be a hostile, aggressive, and generally negative world. In other words, burned out firefighters must learn how to integrate "gray areas" into their thinking, and to remove their egos from the decision-making process. It is necessary to be able to see clear alternatives and develop insight into who we are and how we think and perceive the world. It must be remembered that restructuring one's thinking will allow for a greater sense of well-being, both psychologically and physically, as both these aspects of our lives work together.

Working through a burnout condition requires new learning. For some, it's just learning how to be, that is, how to relax with one's self, as opposed to feeling the need to be doing something all of the time. Reading, taking long walks with a loved one or friend, or just relaxing and doing nothing is healthy. It allows the mind and body to heal by not making additional demands to perform, which, as we have seen, can create or add to an already overloaded mental and physical condition.

Often, individuals gravitate toward firefighting to satisfy a dependency need, especially when they perceive a strong and supportive firefighting organization. The firefighter in burnout must eventually realize that no one will take care of him except himself; no organization, government agency, or person will provide for him, particularly at the level he expects. Much of the cynicism that grows within the firefighter results from his disillusionment with the organization itself, and also from the citizens in the community which he serves.

OCCUPATIONAL AND VOCATIONAL TREATMENT OF BURNOUT

The process of transformation creates anxiety for the firefighter in burnout, for he must now face the challenge of interacting with others without his previous role identity and peer support system.

Firefighters who have received a full service retirement, as opposed to cases of burnout resulting in industrial disability early retirement, often report missing the job to a decreasing extent as the distance in time from their date of retirement   increases.

Those who retire under less favorable, primary stress-related factors of disability (burnout), frequently wait a significant period of time, sometimes six months to a year and a half or longer, before re-entering the labor force. The objective physical aspects of one's disability must be resolved, or at least be in treatment, before an individual can determine what job functions he is physically capable of performing.

A considerable number of burned out firefighters pursue training in areas far different from that of firefighting work. In many states, vocational rehabilitation services and vocational evaluation programs are available to firefighters who receive a disability retirement and/or a favorable worker's compensation case award.

Burnout is devastating for the firefighter who is used to being in a highly active occupation demanding the utmost from them physically and emotionally. The prospect of retirement for these individuals is often as catastrophic as are the experiences on the job. In this regard, it has been my clinical experience that there is no retirement, per se, for firefighters who are no longer actively employed by their respective departments. For in reality, when we do nothing, anticipate nothing, and have established no short or long term goals for ourselves, we begin to die. Life becomes meaningless and devoid of purpose; we vegetate rather than live. There are countless numbers of retirees who, for many of the reasons cited in these pages, find themselves isolated at home alone in front of the television, or at the local pub "killing" the hours of the day, when in reality, there is a slow death going on inside themselves.

COMMENTS ON BURNOUT

The burnout syndrome is more to be avoided than treated. Unless fundamental changes are made in one's attitude, motivations, willingness to communicate needs, wants, and fears; and new potentials and interests are developed outside of the job, the probability that burnout will occur, or remain complete, is high. The concern here is not so much the fear that burnout will reoccur, but rather, that one's authoritarian and dogmatic attitudes will continue throughout one's life in other employment or in retirement. This would overshadow the possibility of interacting in the world with others on a more open and less pressured basis.

It also cannot be over-emphasized that burnout victims had help reaching their state of exhaustion. The occupational demands of firefighting and ongoing departmental pressures create the catalyst for the process of burnout to occur.

From a positive standpoint, burnout can also be growth-producing. While it definitely marks the end of a primary aspect of one's life, for which grieving must take place, it can also herald a new chapter and healthier approach to one's existence. In this regard, overcoming burnout requires for us a reevaluation of our priorities, vocational direction, values, attitudes and life's meaning and purpose. Learning that *balance and moderation are essential for healthy living* must also become an imperative for the victim of burnout.

SUMMARY

FIREFIGHTER BURNOUT

- Burnout isn't dramatic; it's a slow, insidious process that works overtime doing its misery from the inside out

- Burnout is exhaustion

- Burnout affects all aspects of one's life: psychological, physical, work and family

PSYCHOLOGICAL AND EMOTIONAL SIGNS OF BURNOUT

- Psychological exhaustion, including mental fatigue and loss of motivation

- Inability to perceive or generate alternative solutions — loss of positive attitude

- Despair and feeling it takes everything to just get through the day

- Socially withdrawn

- Thoughts related to death and suicide

PHYSICAL SIGNS OF BURNOUT

- Exhaustion — loss of energy and drive

- Physical illness

- Sleeping difficulties

- Muscular tension

OCCUPATIONAL/VOCATIONAL SIGNS OF BURNOUT

- Increased absenteeism
- Low level of morale
- Significant loss of efficiency in work
- Overly personalizing with the job

FAMILY RELATED SIGNS OF BURNOUT

- Feeling distant from loved ones
- Refusing to participate in family or social events
- Verbal or physical abuse of family
- Lack of interest or desire for sexual sharing

TREATMENT OF BURNOUT

- Physical Evaluation
- Professional counseling
- Leave of absence
- Family support
- Peer group interest
- Learning new attitudes and skills
- Reevaluate one's priorities, vocational direction, and attitudes

CHAPTER SEVEN

ALCOHOLISM AND THE FIREFIGHTER

Blaming others, or outside conditions for one's own misbehavior may be the child's privilege; if an adult denies responsibility for his actions, it is another step toward personality disintegration.

Bruno   Bettelheim

There are approximately 100 million people in this country who drink. Many are heavy drinkers, yet only one in ten becomes a problem drinker or an alcoholic. Most alcoholics, incidentally, are not down-and-outers (skid row accounts for less than 5%), but average people desperately trying to ignore their problems or hide them from other people. Or, as seen in many cases of firefighter stress, alcohol is used as a form of *self-medication* to help reduce symptoms of anxiety. Alcoholism cannot be cured, but it can be arrested, and its victims restored to useful lives.[1]

According to The National Council on Alcoholism, approximately 10% of all employees nationwide suffer from alcoholism. Each alcoholic employee costs his company, conservatively estimated, 25% of his salary in absenteeism, (usually 25% of salary is lost to absenteeism alone), tardiness, spoiled materials, reduced efficiency and effectiveness, on-the-job accidents and medical benefits.[2]

Using the National Council's figure of 10% and adding a 5% buffer, the alcoholic firefighter, with an annual salary of $25,000, would alone cost his department $3,750 a year. In a department of 100 employees, the expected annual performance loss would be $375,000.

For the untreated alcoholic firefighter, termination is inevitable. As his dependence on alcohol increases, his impaired judgment and adverse public image create a condition of liability not only for the firefighter and his department, but for the public he is sworn to serve.

PSYCHOLOGICAL, EMOTIONAL, AND PHYSICAL SIGNS OF ALCOHOLISM

Clinical treatment experience has shown that it is relatively easy to get an alcoholic sober. Keeping him sober and comfortable with his sobriety is a far more complex matter!

A combination of steps are involved in reaching and maintaining an alcoholic's sobriety. Yet, each alcoholic is different. Therefore, treatment depends on their emotional problems, including the length of time the firefighter has been addicted to alcohol, attitude of the family toward alcohol, and most important, *his willingness to deal with the disorder*.[3]

If left untreated or ignored, alcoholism causes negative effects. These are: lowered job efficiency, poor work quality, increased vehicular, and other types of accidents (both on and off duty), breakdown of family relationships, impaired interpersonal relations, and deterioration of physical health. Psychological and emotional instability, resulting from alcoholism, produces self-destructive behaviors which may also result in suicide.

EARLY SIGNS OF ALCOHOLISM

Memory blackout, feelings of guilt, and aggressive behavior, accompanied by an increasing tolerance to and dependency on alcohol, are crucial warning signals of an alcohol problem.

Physically, the alcoholic firefighter may begin to show a weight gain, red eyes, flushed face, and tremors of the hands. In addition, a decrease of sexual desire and poor sexual performance, often fuels existing marital and family tensions. These dysfunctional characteristics lead to an increase of alcohol consumption, thereby creating a vicious circle for the alcoholic firefighter.

The effects of a hangover, such as excessive thirst, headache, fatigue, nausea, jitters and tremors, create a miserable post-drinking experience for the alcoholic. Unfortunately, however, not miserable enough to eliminate his desire to drink. Aspirin and large amounts of coffee are consumed in an attempt to counteract the painful and debilitating effects of the hangover condition. When all else fails, a morning drink of alcohol becomes routine.

Deterioration of work performance is usually noted. Lateness, lack of motivation at work, fantasies and daydreams of escaping one's life situation, being easily distracted, slowed reflexes, distorted eye-hand coordination, and impaired visual and psychological discrimination, are also evident in the work-life of the alcoholic. A comprehensive overview of the signs and symptoms of alcoholism is presented below.

SIGNS AND SYMPTOMS OF ALCOHOL ABUSE AMONG FIREFIGHTERS

PRIMARY SYMPTOMS OF ALCOHOLISM

- Memory black-out during an alcoholic episode
- Constant preoccupation with alcohol and alcohol-related activities
- Increasing tolerance to alcohol
- Psychological and physical dependency upon alcohol

PORTRAIT OF A WORKING ALCOHOLIC

OCCUPATIONAL SIGNS

- Absenteeism, including "partial" absences and excessive use of sick leave
- Vehicular and other types of "accidents"
- Deterioration of work performance
- Physical Signs
- Weight gain not attributable to overeating
- Red, bleary eyes
- Hand tremor
- Excessive sweating — may reek of alcohol through the pores of the skin

- Flushed face

- Increased jitteryness

- Decreased sexual desire

- Lack of appetite while drinking and a craving for "sweets"

- Instances of loss of sexual potency or inability to maintain an erection

- Decreased motor reflexes

- Sleep disorder — feeling unrested and tired when awakening

- Suffering from hangover

- Thirst, headache, fatigue, jitters, nausea

- Excessive use of aspirin, black coffee, and other stimulants to counteract overwhelming fatigue; if this fails, a morning drink of alcohol to dull the effects and quiet the nerves

NEUROLOGICAL SIGNS

- Impaired visual discrimination

- Loss of recent and long-term memory

- Increased irritability

- Problems with abstract thinking. In time, thinking becomes very concrete as memory and recall diminish

PSYCHOLOGICAL AND EMOTIONAL SIGNS

- Irritable, hostile, impulsive, demanding, cynical

- Very low threshold for tolerating frustration

- Moody and frequently showing signs of depression and anxiety

- Emotionally unstable — up one minute, down the next

- Profound personality change

- Marital and family problems

- Loss of meaning and purpose in life

- Rational thinking is significantly effected

- Moral judgment is compromised

THE PERSONALITY OF THE ALCOHOLIC FIREFIGHTER

There are many common personality features among alcoholics. Alcoholics remain emotionally fixated at the approximate age they actively began practicing their addiction. Significant among all alcoholics is their ability to rationalize their use of alcohol. Guilt and self-condemnation can be buried by another drink.

Among the chemically dependent, behaviors often reminiscent of earlier stages of development are frequently displayed during an alcoholic acting-out episode. As adults, these individuals often reveal themselves through a see-sawing of emotions and a desire to desensitize themselves from their fearful mistrust of others. They also distance themselves emotionally in their interpersonal relationships.

Despite their efforts to drown feelings and desires with the use of alcohol, there is usually a recurrent experience of **anxiety** and **mood swings**, primarily manifested and experienced as depression and persistent indefinable fears. The alcoholic often displays persistent self-doubt regarding his strengths and aptitudes, and frequently avoids self-directed or self-initiated behavior. Most notable about this personality is a search for supportive persons or institutions upon which to depend, such as job, family, or a dating relationship. However, the individual's desire to satisfy both his strong dependency needs as well as his need for independence and autonomy often creates a conflict resulting in total loss of relationship and/or divorce. This appears to be very common among alcoholic members of the firefighting population, and certainly compounds the stress they experience as part of their personal and work lives.

Many alcoholics repress their need for acceptance from others by maintaining a good measure of emotional distance. They learn that by fading into the social background, by assuming passive roles and a willingness to follow the direction of others, they are able to keep the pressure off themselves, while at the same time remaining safe from anticipated humiliation and rejection. The passive lifestyle of the alcoholic is partially defensive, but also stems from general fatigue due to depleted energy from the abuse of alcohol. As the disease progresses, there is also progressive deterioration of their physical conditions.

The alcoholic may appear moderately depressed, pessimistic of the future, worried, often feeling as though some ominous event is about to occur which will further add to his misery. Moral decay and the loss of spiritual values further compounds the inadequate self-concept of the alcoholic.

ALCOHOLISM AND PERSONALITY CHANGES

Marked personality changes when drinking are a significant feature of the alcoholic personality. The quiet, shy firefighter becomes more outgoing, sometimes exhibiting aggressive behavior. Suddenly he feels better about himself. The alcohol is working! The alcohol frees the passive and dependent individual from his self-imposed emotional and social inhibitions. The price paid after an episode of insobriety may be guilt and remorse for statements and behaviors acted out while intoxicated.

The sarcastic, angry firefighter may become violent, acting out his aggression in ways that display the poor judgment of the alcoholic when intoxicated. He may also exhibit uncharacteristic emotionality and remorse for his actions resulting from the breakdown of psychological defenses while drunk.

Firefighters who are alcoholics may also become heavy-handed with victims as well as easily frustrated with the public in general. They may act in an authoritarian, nonsupportivemanner, when just the opposite attitude would have been more appropriate. They may act out their frustrations and guilt with loved ones as well. Even their best friend can become the brunt of their hostility. *No one is spared the devastating consequences of alcohol use and abuse.*

The acting out of unacceptable impulses forces the chemically dependent individual to withdraw emotionally even more into his feelings of guilt, shame, and remorse. **Denial** becomes the ultimate defense necessary to preserve the alcoholic's sense of self-esteem.

Depression is often the primary emotional experience of the alcoholic. These individuals may not be aware that through self-medication with alcohol to reduce the effects of their anxiety, they are, in fact, creating the primary cause of their depression, thereby further reinforcing their dependency upon alcohol.

In the fire department, alcoholic firefighters reinforce one another's behavior and chemical dependency. They find acceptance with others like themselves as they gradually begin to experience alienation from the outside world. This alienation from family and friends often results from acting out impulses verbally and physically. At the same time, they believe that they are reasonable and rational. That, however, is not the case.

As we all know, you can not reason with a drunk! The loss of good judgment seals the sense of guilt felt by the alcoholic as his disease progresses.

As previously mentioned, alcohol use and abuse is commonly practiced in fire departments as a means of self-medicating, to relieve or reduce sensations of anxiety and emotional tension. Additionally, for rookies, drinking is a way of gaining acceptance and approval from senior firefighters.

The internal experience of the alcoholic is one of a lonely and slowly deteriorating, living hell. He feels as though no one understands him. He believes that he has no control or responsibility over his life, causing him to feel even more helpless and depressed.

The emotional dependency needs are often as great for the alcoholic as are his chemical needs, since he fears going through his "journey of horror" alone. This accounts for the fact that alcoholics frequently maintain multiple relationships in order to satisfy their emotional dependency needs as well. By so doing, they further reinforce their lack of independence and personal freedom to do and be who they are.

ADDITIONAL FEATURES OF ALCOHOLISM

Neurologically, there may be losses of recent and long-term memory, and a general dulling of the intellect. As the alcoholism progresses, memory loss increases. In an effort to compensate for the memory loss, the alcoholic may "mentally create" a picture in his mind of what he thought actually occurred during a blackout.

The alcoholic also may appear irritable and hostile. He can also be impulsive and demanding. "I don't have a problem," he proclaims. Rather, he blames others for his ills and displaces his frustration and aggression onto them, in lieu of accepting the responsibility for his own actions.

The combination of the dependent personality struggling for independence and deeply repressed anger is a major aspect of the alcoholic's psychological make-up.

Financial problems abound among alcohol-dependent firefighters. True to form, blame or responsibility for their "condition" is displaced to others, or to alleged circumstances beyond their control.

ALCOHOLICS AND THEIR RELATIONSHIPS

The chemically dependent firefighter may be in a relationship with a spouse or significant other who may also deny the existence of the dependency and the insidious effects caused by the addiction itself. Often, the spouse of the alcoholic may be passive and emotionally dependent upon his/her mate. Fearful of saying anything about chemical abuse which would create further disharmony within the family or relationship, they give quiet or implied approval of the excesses they are frequently required to observe or participate in.

At some point, however, the spouse or "friend" of the chemically dependent firefighter proclaims they "can't take it any longer!" Criticism is often met with violent outbursts or further withdrawal on the part of the chemically dependent firefighter. The spouse or "friend" may no longer want to go along for the ride. They may no longer continue to play the role of the accepting, and dependency reinforcing, co-alcoholic.

The spouse of the alcoholic becomes frustrated and tired of being forced into the dual role of mother and father, because the alcoholic relinquishes all family responsibility, often taking the position that being a firefighter is demanding enough of his time and energy.

This is the crossroads of the relationship. It is at this point that the relationship is in jeopardy of disintegrating. Either a cry for help goes out, or a change in living arrangements ensues. When the co-alcoholic begins to recognize his participation, the scenario, out of necessity, changes. New ground rules must then be established.

TREATING THE ALCOHOLIC FIREFIGHTER

As has been shown thus far, alcoholism is a compulsive disorder which undermines the very core of existence for the alcoholic and affects all of those around him. Alcoholism is a powerful disease which leaves in its wake victims who frequently feel helpless and powerless to change their situation. For the alcoholic firefighter, problems associated with gaining awareness that the disease exists are compounded by the fact that alcohol consumption is such an integral part of the firefighter's culture. Drinking, for many firefighters, is an occupational expectation or requirement. It is also a primary means of socializing and "unstressing" after a shift.

At the present time, there is no known cause of alcoholism. However, current thinking equates alcoholism to a hereditary allergic reaction. It appears that alcoholism runs in families, and may result from a genetic predisposition to the disease. There is also a social learning aspect to alcoholism as well. From my clinical experience, the majority of those treated for primary alcoholism had a significant role model who also suffered from this compulsive disorder. Consequently, drinking alcohol for some is like playing Russian roulette, since no one knows who is sensitized to the disease and who is not. Unfortunately, these individuals will not be aware that they are sensitive until after the condition has been established and its insidious negative effects have begun.

OVERCOMING DENIAL

The *disease* of alcoholism is so powerful, and its effects so profound, that there are preconditions that must be met before any attempt to change can occur or be effective for any length of time.

For the alcoholic firefighter, *breaking through the defense pattern of denial and accepting responsibility for behavior and feelings is mandatory before change can occur.* Generally, for this to happen, a combination of feedback or confrontation about one's drinking behavior, coupled with the alcoholic becoming sick and tired of feeling sick and tired, may become necessary.

Life is often meaningless and empty for the alcoholic, at least until the next drink. Alcoholism is like being tied to a mobile life support system, and without it, on a deep emotional level, many alcoholics believe they don't exist. The alcohol frees them from the emotional inhibition which often causes them to mask a significant part of their personality; alcohol allows these individuals to loosen up. It is often this free, unstressed feeling that further reinforces the process of denial.

Thus, dealing effectively with the alcoholic firefighter, out of necessity, requires an overhaul of his mental approach to life and a change in his pattern of living.

ALCOHOL TREATMENT APPROACHES

There is no one approach or specific treatment plan that has been shown to be effective in each and every case of alcoholism, since all firefighters suffering from alcoholism will not all be at the same stage or level of their addiction at the same time.

There are many approaches that have been found to be effective in working with an alcoholic and his family, which may also include treating a spouse or other family member for alcoholism as well.

Many of the approaches previously discussed may be used in the treatment of alcoholism at the discretion of the professionals working with the addicted firefighter. The goal of the alcohol treatment plan, developed on a case by case basis, must consider the specific needs of the firefighter and the needs of those closest to him.

Since alcohol treatment approaches have previously been discussed, other key features employed in the treatment of alcoholism will be highlighted. Further, since there may be significant occupational factors related to a firefighter's alcoholism, department interventions are also presented in outline form as a part of a comprehensive plan. It must be emphasized that a professional therapist or member of a department's alcohol or stress program be consulted, as support and assistance is vital to increase the likelihood of a sustained recovery. The following is an outline of a comprehensive alcohol treatment plan:

Break Through the Pattern of Psychological Denial — There can be no sustained recovery while denial is present. The treatment of alcoholism is facilitated only when the individual is able to recognize that he is suffering from a disease. As long as he is actively dealing with his disease, he needn't feel ashamed or stigmatized.

Detoxification — When the firefighter or family

member feels he is unable to stop the use or abuse of alcohol on his own, or his condition is so deteriorated that custodial care becomes necessary, an inpatient detoxification program under medical supervision is the treatment of choice. These programs most often require a 28-day in-hospital stay. Medical evaluation may include the prescribing of antabuse and/or tranquilizers. Definitely follow-up with programs including A.A., Alanon, Alateen, Adult Children of Alcoholics (A.C.A).

Diet and Exercise − Facilitate the release of stress and help to reverse the effects of depression.

Counseling and Psychotherapy − Primary among the goals of counseling should be the development of insight, self-awareness, self-acceptance and ego strengthening. Deal with issues related to emotional dependency and repressed anger. Learn to balance emotions and function effectively at the feeling level. Deprogram your belief system, especially thoughts related to low self-worth. It is important to begin seeing "the cup as half-full rather than half-empty." You must be responsible for who and how you are. Through communication, begin to allow others to know you on a deeper level. This allows us to begin to know ourselves better. We can then begin to share ourselves with others more freely. It also helps to make life a less lonely journey.

Deal with the symbolic meaning of alcohol − i.e., "Liquid Love." How does alcohol fit into the historical pattern of your life?

Focus on the chronological age at which chemical abuse began to be acted out − By so doing, emotional growth can be charted from that point.

Learn compassion and healthy self-love, rather than using alcohol to compensate for feelings of low self-worth.

Assertion Training — Facilitates the building of self-confidence, self-acceptance, and teaches how to discharge anger, negative thoughts and feelings effectively. It also defines the limits of who we are by helping us to understand what we will and will not accept as part of our life. We affirm who we are through assertion training methods. It helps provide a clearer picture of who we are both to ourselves and others.

Relaxation Training — Progressive relaxation, hypnosis and self-hypnosis, visual imagery techniques.

Family Counseling and Therapy — Spouse's addictive disorder, if any, should be uncovered and dealt with. Address issues related to spouse's dependency, passivity, and "co-alcoholism." Explore the dynamics of the family in light of the alcoholic's disorder; how each family member feels about it and how they see it affecting the entire family structure and system of functioning.

Develop a Spiritual Awareness — Not necessarily of a religious nature, which is an important aspect of many treatment plans. The goal of a spiritual awareness to see a higher meaning and purpose to life, and that you are not alone in the world.

Develop an Awareness of the Compulsive Nature of One's Personality — For many chemically-dependent individuals the compulsive aspects of one's personality must be explored and behavior and feelings dealt with so that alcohol use and abuse is not replaced by some other form of dependency need that does not enhance the self, such as compulsive eating or spending.

DEPARTMENTAL INTERVENTIONS FOR THE IDENTIFICATION AND TREATMENT OF ALCOHOLISM

The following model of an alcoholism intervention program may be employed by any fire department. Individual aspects of this model may be used or integrated within an existing stress unit or employee assistance program for the identification and treatment of alcoholism. The model assumes that there is either a full time professional or a team of trained personnel who are available to implement the goals and objectives of a departmental program. Above all else, for an intervention program to be effective, trust must be established between the employee assistance program staff and the department and employees who might avail themselves of this service. The department or employer must provide a nonthreatening approach to the identification and treatment of the alcoholic employee.

PROGRAM OBJECTIVES

- Retain valuable and experienced employees through positive approaches to emotional and behavioral problems associated with alcoholism and occupational stress.

- Restore productivity through early identification of employee distress.

- Decrease annual costs to the department as a result of effective intervention methods.

METHODS NECESSARY TO ACCOMPLISH OBJECTIVES

- Develop Knowledge of Community Resources and Referral Services — Outside resources must have hands-on knowledge of firefighters and occupational stress factors related to fire fighting.

- Identify the Alcoholic Employee — Referral should be made to appropriate resources within the department, or to appropriate outside resources, especially for medical evaluation.

- Develop Peer Counseling Program.

- Develop Recovering A.A. Group.

- Publicize names of department staff members who have had specific training in alcoholism stress awareness counseling and are familiar with crisis intervention methods.

- Use members of the Employee Assistance Program as a consultation resource to management.

- Develop a training program to motivate supervisors of alcoholic employees to seek assistance.

- Develop follow-up studies to determine the effectiveness of Department Alcohol Intervention Program.

- Be involved in recruit screening process and psychological testing.

- Develop workshops for management on methods of dealing with the families of alcoholic and chemically dependent personnel.

EXPECTED OUTCOMES OF AN ALCOHOLISM INTERVENTION PROGRAM

- Increase in job performance, efficiency, and quality of work.

- Decrease in absenteeism, including use of sick leave and medical benefits.

- Increase in employee morale and personal job satisfaction.

- Decrease costs to the department from more efficient and effective use of personnel.

- Decrease medical costs to the employer.

- Decrease injuries sustained on and off duty.

- Incur fewer suspensions and disciplinary actions.

- Decrease management time spent on disciplinary cases.

- Improve public image due to less negative contacts with citizens.

- Increase intra-departmental communication.

- Increase accountability with regard to program effectiveness.

References

1. International Association of Machinists and Aerospace Workers. *Occupational Alcoholism Programs Thru Union Contracts.* Washington, D.C.

2. National Council On Alcoholism, Inc. *Business, Industry And Time In A Bottle.* Los Angeles: Los Angeles County Office On Alcohol Abuse & Alcoholism.

3. Ibid.

Additional Resources

Alcoholics Anonymous Headquarters,
General Service Office
Box 459, Grand Central Station
New York, NY 10017

National Clearinghouse for Alcohol Information
Box 2345
Rockville, M.D. 20852

The National Council on Alcoholism
Two Park Avenue South
New York, NY 10016

SUMMARY

ALCOHOLISM AND THE FIREFIGHTER

It is estimated that 10% of the American work force is affected by alcoholism. Therefore, one can predict that at least ten percent of firefighter personnel would be chemically dependent and be in different stages of the disease of alcoholism at any point in time.

PORTRAIT OF THE WORKING ALCOHOLIC

Occupational signs:
- Absenteeism and accidents

Physical signs:
- Red, bleary eyes, flushed face, tremors

- Hangover symptoms of headache, jitters, thirst

- Excessive use of: aspirin, black coffee, and other stimulants

Neurological signs:
- Memory loss

- Blackouts

- Motor impairment

- Impaired vision

- Loss of recent and long-term memory

- Dulling of intelligence

- Psychological and emotional signs:

- Irritable, hostile, impulsive behavior

- Loss of meaning and purpose

- Marital and family problems

THE ALCOHOLIC PERSONALITY

In general, alcoholics remain emotionally fixated at the approximate age they actively began practicing their addiction.

ALCOHOLICS EXPERIENCE

- Acting out episodes during drinking

- Individual self-doubt

- Need for acceptance by others

- Behavioral change

- Denial

- Emotional seesaw between euphoria and depression

- Loss of spiritual values and beliefs

TREATMENT OF ALCOHOLISM

- Seek the help of a professional
- Individual counseling
- Assertion training
- Detoxification
- Diet and exercise

CHAPTER EIGHT

ORGANIZATIONAL CONTRIBUTIONS TO FIREFIGHTER STRESS

There is nothing sacred about tradition . . . The brain carries the memory of yesterday, which is tradition, and is frightened to let go, because it cannot face something new. Tradition becomes our security; and when the mind is secure, it is in decay.

Krishnamurti

Every organization has forces within it that result in employee stress. Organizational stress in the fire service pertains to those forces within a department that are "always present" and operate so that not only the department as a whole but the community they serve pays dearly.

There are aspects of firefighting that generate anxiety, crisis, or trauma. As most firefighters know, and would readily agree, there are also internal departmental factors that create or intensify emotional distress within its employees. Graph 1 illustrates the results of a 1987 study[1] which indicated the major complaint regarding occupational stress among public sector employees was attributed to "job pressures."

The purpose of this chapter is to emphasize the need for a heightened awareness of existing organizational stress factors, early detection and intervention of stress among employees, and most importantly, the need to work toward the elimination of intra-departmental stress conditions. Firefighting is labor intensive. This is supported by the fact that approximately 90% of any department's annual budget is spent on its personnel. It stands to reason that it would be cost effective to prevent stress-related disorders. Many departments and agencies today treat stress on a purely crisis intervention basis. By addressing departmental factors instead, the problem of organizational stress can be dealt with directly. Due to the paramilitary nature of firefighting, with its rigid chain of command and negative system of reinforcement, there are certain stress factors that will not and cannot be changed. Some factors, which are unique to a particular department, can be changed to the benefit of all, once detected.

The level of morale within a department is a significant indicator of employee satisfaction and also provides an index of employee productivity. Consequently, the greater the employee morale, the higher the payoff to the entire department and the population it serves.

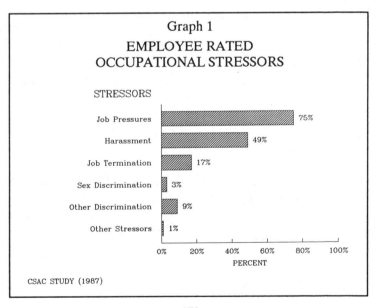

Graph 1
EMPLOYEE RATED
OCCUPATIONAL STRESSORS

STRESSORS

Job Pressures	75%
Harassment	49%
Job Termination	17%
Sex Discrimination	3%
Other Discrimination	9%
Other Stressors	1%

0% 20% 40% 60% 80% 100%
PERCENT

CSAC STUDY (1987)

LACK OF MANAGERIAL SKILLS AS A FACTOR OF STRESS

The profession of firefighting has grown from a volunteer organization with those administrators proving themselves on the fire ground and in the political arena of the organization itself. In the past, coming up through the ranks meant growing by experience and self-education. There was little emphasis on formal education, nor prescribed methods of training for up-and-coming officers. The importance of training and education has grown in recent years, especially in relation to managerial skills. There is a general recognition of the increased need for complex communication, personnel, fire ground and political systems management. Today's manager cannot simply couple his innate ability to lead with his years of experience. He must now be a manager of people and resources who must expertly interpose with all phases of local, state and federal government. He must communicate well with his subordinates and superiors, not only verbally but also in writing.

Stress in the fire service occurs when there is a conflict between the older administrators who are locked into their outdated methods of managing, and the younger, educated firefighters trained to understand the complexities of management. The older firefighters want the comfort of the familiar ways of handling problems. The newer firefighters expect a more professional approach to handling problems. Innovations in technology and advanced systems management concepts are rapidly coming to the forefront in public administration as the need to do more with less becomes an economic reality. In the past, fire administrators have been able to say that theirs is a "technically special" department requiring skills that do not generally apply to public administration practices. The reality is fire department managers seldom fight fires. They spend most of their time managing people and resources, communicating with superiors and subordinates. Hence, today's firefighter manager needs a base of knowledge regarding the political, social, and economic environment; managerial processes; analytical tools; individual, group, and organizational behavior; Equal Opportunity Employment; Affirmative Action; Worker's Compensation; Computer Skills. Without this base of knowledge, the fire manager feels the stress of incompetence and struggles to make modern decisions based on experiences in an antiquated management system. This stress is also felt by the new firefighter as he cannot communicate well with the older managers. The new firefighter knows there is something wrong but is forced by tradition to mold his style to that of his superiors. Any thought of change on the part of the new firefighter is usually met with, "You haven't been on the job long enough to comment."

COLLECTIVE BARGAINING AND EMPLOYEE STRESS

In 1969, the Meyers-Milias-Brown Act granted public employees the right to labor union representation and collective bargaining. Since then, employee morale in many departments has been significantly affected by an "us against them" labor-management relationship, especially when contract negotiations and other agreements cannot be satisfactorily conducted. In many cases, the constant pressure of these two factions "bucking horns" in an adversarial way has been seen as an added stressor in the lives of many firefighters.

ORGANIZATIONAL STRESS FACTORS

In the following section, a number of factors primarily related to organizational stress are presented. This listing is not meant to be all inclusive. My experience indicates that every department has its own unique conditions which significantly affect employee morale. In general, the following factors apply to the profession of firefighter and relate to employee stress.

- **Labor-Management Friction** — Creates significant ongoing stress and may result in employee burnout.

- **Excessive Paperwork** — Firefighters are inundated with paperwork; reports, record keeping, and other such bureaucratic requirements add a dimension to the occupation of firefighting that many fire officers have difficulty coping with. While the basic and essential functions of firefighting remain to be carried out, the additional "paper load" serves as an added stressor for many fire officers. Officers question the necessity of such record keeping. In time, many fire officers begin to question the validity of their own work efforts, and, due to the fact that they over-identify with their profession, in time, begin to question their own self-worth as well as their worth to the organization.

- **Poor Detection and Management of Stress Related Disorders** — Fire administrators also suffer from the effects of stress. However, unlike firefighters below the level of captain, command personnel are expected to perform in an exemplary manner despite their own emotional and psychological problems. From my clinical experience, members of administration do not typically avail themselves of stress management services to the same extent that firefighters do. Therefore, many fire administrators function on a less than adequate level due to their own stress-related problems. This can compromise their judgment and managerial ability.

- **Loss of "Soft Jobs" to Civilian Employees** — In many departments, there is a growing trend toward placing civilian employees in positions once occupied by firefighting personnel. Many of these "inside" or "soft" positions were available to firefighters who were experiencing stress and needed a change from their regular assignment. With these positions now handled by civilians, firefighters feel that there is no place for them to temporarily hide while they attempt to deal with their stress.

- **Fire Station Assignment by the Seniority Bid System** — Older firefighters, due to their seniority, often elect to spend the latter part of their career in slower fire stations. Thus, firefighters who are approaching burnout cannot decrease their level of activity and stress or recuperate in the slower station, because "resting spots" are frequently occupied.

- **Hiring Individuals Who Do Not Meet Standard Employment Criteria or Lowering Standards To Satisfy Racial Minority Quotas** — Incompetent employees are seen as a management problem if employment standards are compromised, especially due to poor screening and training programs at the recruit   level.

- **Inability to Tolerate Enforced Idleness** — Although many firefighters might attribute over-work as a principal cause of stress, idleness can be seen as a factor of occupational stress. Having little to do for a 24-hour period can be very stressful for some firefighters who thrive on high activity.

STRESS AND CARDIAC ILLNESS

Frequently, stress manifests itself in cardiac disorders. A recent study of occupational retirements in the fire service,[2] found heart disease to be the primary factor of occupational disability and employee death. The results of that study are presented in Graph 2 below.

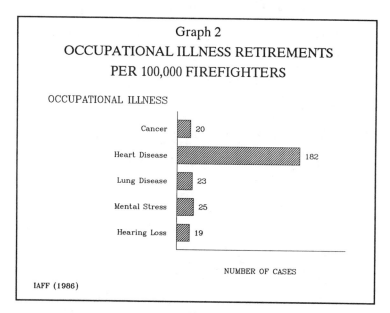

Graph 2
OCCUPATIONAL ILLNESS RETIREMENTS
PER 100,000 FIREFIGHTERS

OCCUPATIONAL ILLNESS

Cancer	20
Heart Disease	182
Lung Disease	23
Mental Stress	25
Hearing Loss	19

NUMBER OF CASES

IAFF (1986)

An early comprehensive study of firefighter work injuries and illness[3] indicated that considerable experimental and clinical evidence has shown that the following factors, more common to firefighters than the general male population, are predisposing in the causation of severe cardiac disorders:

- Stress of firefighting

- Environmental stress (heat and cold)

- Trauma and shock

- Burns

- Inhalation of smoke and gases (including carbon monoxide)

The following recommendations are herein offered for departments to consider for the reduction of cardiovascular deaths as well as other stress-related illness to firefighters:

- Careful selection, pre-employment physical and laboratory tests

- Annual re-examination

- Enforced "No Smoking" restrictions

- Weight control programs

- Diet control program, including a diet low in saturated fats

- Physical fitness program, emphasizing endurance-type physical exercise

- Improved respiratory equipment

- Supplying safety officers at all fires

- Monitoring stress under "combat conditions"

- Mandatory post-trauma debriefing for all involved in a major catastrophe

- Regular physical examinations can be used to detect changes in EKG's and blood pressure

- Triglyceride levels can be modified by diet and medication

Firehouse diets, that meet medically established guidelines, have been advocated as a means of combating heart disease. One problem that might arise with special firehouse diets is — who will pay for the food. Firefighters now buy their own food but are free to choose what they will eat. Another consideration is that the hoped for effects of the diet might be obviated by the type of food eaten by firefighters on their days off.

Another program already instituted by many fire departments is participation by firefighters in sports, physical training, and exercise. These activities develop muscular strength, flexibility, agility, and stamina, which are necessary physical characteristics for firefighters. Sports activities develop some of these characteristics but probably to a lesser extent than physical training programs designed to meet fitness objectives. Among the activities that will produce a training effect are running, swimming, and cycling.

In conclusion, the structure of the organization contributes greatly to firefighter stress. At present, not enough is being done. Fortunately, organizations can be changed through awareness, education and a conscious effort on the part of management to reduce those conditions which create stress.

References

1. International Association of Firefighters, Department of Occupational Health and Safety. *1986 Annual Death and Injury Survey*. Washington, D. C.: International Association of Firefighters, 1986.

2. Ibid.

3. California Department of Industrial Relations, Division of Labor Statistics and Research. *Work Injuries and Illness To Local Firefighters In California*. San Francisco: Division of Labor Statistics and Research, 1977.

SUMMARY

Every organization has forces within it that result in employee stress.

LACK OF MANAGERIAL SKILLS AS A FACTOR OF STRESS

Stress in the fire service occurs when there is a conflict between the older administrators who are locked into their past methods of managing, and the younger firefighters who understand the complexities of management.

TODAY'S FIREFIGHTER MANAGER NEEDS A BASE OF KNOWLEDGE

- He must be a manager of people and resources
- Expertly interpose with local, state and federal government
- Communicate well with his subordinates and superiors
- Political, social, and economic environment
- Managerial processes
- Individual, group, and organizational behavior
- Equal Opportunity Employment, Affirmative Action, Worker's Compensation
- Computer Skills

COLLECTIVE BARGAINING AND EMPLOYEE STRESS

The Meyers-Milias-Brown Act of 1969 granted public employees the right to labor union representation and collective bargaining. Since then, employee morale in many departments has been significantly affected by an "us against them" labor-management relationship.

ORGANIZATIONAL FACTORS PRIMARILY RELATED TO EMPLOYEE STRESS

- Labor-management friction
- Excessive paperwork
- Poor detection and management of stress-related disorders
- Loss of "soft jobs" to civilian employees
- Fire station assignment by the seniority bid system
- Hiring individuals who do not meet standard employment
- Inability to tolerate enforced idleness

STRESS AND CARDIAC ILLNESS

Frequently, stress manifests itself in cardiac disorders:

- Stress of firefighting
- Environmental stress (heat and cold)
- Trauma and shock

- Burns
- Inhalation of smoke and gases (including carbon monoxide)

RECOMMENDATIONS FOR REDUCTION OF CARDIOVASCULAR DEATHS AND OTHER STRESS-RELATED ILLNESS

- Careful selection, pre-employment physical and laboratory tests
- Annual re-examination
- Enforced "No Smoking" restrictions
- Weight control programs
- Diet control program, including a diet low in saturated fats
- Physical fitness program, emphasizing endurance-type physical exercise
- Improved respiratory equipment
- Supplying safety officers at all fires
- Monitoring stress under "combat conditions"
- Mandatory post-trauma debriefing for all involved in a major catastrophe
- Regular physical examinations can be used to detect changes in EKG's and blood pressure
- Triglyceride levels can be modified by diet and medication

CHAPTER NINE

STRESS AND RETIREMENT

He who has a why to live can bear with almost any how.
Nietzsche

W hat will I do, what can I do?" "Who and where are my friends?" "Who cares about me?" "Does anyone understand what is happening to me?" These are but a few of the thoughts which parade, sometimes obsessively, through the mind of the firefighter facing retirement. For the occupationally injured firefighter in the midst of a disability retirement, the pressures and uncertainty, especially about the future, are great, and the fears enormous.

Prior to the realization that retirement was approaching, there was definite purpose for the firefighter. He had friends he could count on. He had a reason to get up every day and he interacted with his peers in a generally comfortable and predictable fashion.

In retirement, his predictable world becomes all mixed up; mental and emotional confusion are prominent while awake and asleep. To compound the situation, those upon whom the firefighter used to count on for camaraderie, now avoid him should he happen by the firehouse.

The firefighter in the throws of the retirement process knows, so well, how past retirees were merely tolerated. They were felt, by many of the active firefighters, to have little to contribute to the organization. In reality, the retired firefighter has little to offer other than an anxious hint, for the active firefighter, of the potentiality of his own fate upon retirement.

In essence, retiring from the fire department is like getting a divorce; separating for the good and mutual benefit of all. No longer able to go back to the "good old days", as if, in reality, they ever existed anyway.

A Battalion Chief, with twenty-six years experience in a moderate size fire department in a community of 65,000, summed up his perception of the many firefighters he has seen retire throughout his career:

When you retire, the first month or so you don't realize you are retired. It could be a month's vacation and you're going to come back. All of a sudden you wake up one day and you realize I'm not going back. Twenty-five years of your life . . . it's not an 8-hour a day job, its a 24-hour a day job. We eat lunch together, we eat dinner together, you go to bed together, you shower together, you get up, you go out and save lives together. It's as big a part of your life as your home life because of the amount of time that you spend here with these people. Three months of the year, 4 months of the year, you're away from your own family and you're here.

Its like when you were single and you had a group of guys you ran around with and one of the guys got married, he was no longer one of the group. He's an outcast. That's exactly what it is here. He's an outcast, he's retired, he's gone and he doesn't know how to get back in. He doesn't fit any longer with the guys that are here because he can't talk about the day to day things. The only things he can talk about are the things that have happened in the past, not the current things.

Maybe they try to make friends on the outside, and they say, "What did you do for a living?" "I was a fireman." Well, now you're out! There are more than a few that are still lost out there, that really haven't taken control of their lives and gone into something new. And that usually occurs because they haven't planned for retirement.

You're here on a day-to-day basis and retirement never comes, its always 10 years away. And all of a sudden you wake up one day and its here. Now its time to turn in your badge and leave. And you haven't prepared yourself. They've got their homes, their cars and things but they haven't prepared for all the idle time. And the first month or two they're fixing-up the house, etc. and when the house and everything has been repaired now what do you do? Yeah, I'm going to play golf everyday, that's what they say. Guys that are golfers say they're going to play 3-4 times a week. Who are you going to play with? Most of the people are out there are making livings, they don't have the time, or if they are out there playing, they probably have 10 times more money than you and they're in a different social status.

We've got a few guys who have moved out of the state. One guy bought an orchard, takes care of his trees. In his mind, he's still worth something, he's still making money, he's productive, he's doing something. And that's the hardest thing for a fireman. Usually they're here working a 24 hour shift, a lot of times they have a job on the side, and they're constantly producing. How do you cut that off and all of a sudden do nothing? Retirement is not sitting back on your front porch and rocking back and forth on your chair anymore.

PSYCHOLOGICAL ISSUES RELATED TO RETIREMENT

It is a reality in our society that the non-working individual considers himself, and is thought, by many members of society, to be out of the main stream of life. The following psychological issues are generally seen among those firefighters who are facing or are in the process of retiring from their occupation.

- Feelings of inadequacy and low self worth seem to go hand in hand with lack of employment. Most of us derive much of our self concept and self-esteem from what we do for a living. Nowhere is this more evident than in firefighter work.

- The need for control and the inability to deal with ambiguity are characteristics of the firefighter personality. The fear of loss of control and uncertainty about the future are felt by many new retirees.

- There is generally the erroneous belief that retirement means enforced idleness.

- Fears of isolation from society.

- How will society view me?

- What does one do with their compulsive work habits upon retirement?

POINTERS FOR SURVIVING RETIREMENT

The following suggestions are derived directly from my

psychotherapeutic work with countless individuals going through the retirement process; from the filing of the initial retirement papers to turning in their ID, and the aftermath.

- Maintain a positive survival spirit. Remember that life is proactive-always moving forward. Learn to live in the present. To remain "stuck" in the past can lead to or signify depression or frustration with ones new life.

- Upon retirement, limit all additional life changes for a period of time — 6 months to one year. Remember that each life change requires us to adapt to those changes and creates more stress for ourselves.

- Overcoming the "Poor Me" attitude upon retirement takes serious effort. One cannot grow from self-pity. In time, others tire of hearing about it anyway.

- Must learn to overcome thoughts and resulting feelings of inadequacy and low self worth.

- Retirement does not have to mean forced idleness. Compulsive work patterns are frequently a sign of other psychological problems as well, such as running away from one's own psychological issues. At times **we must learn to do nothing.** Doing nothing is actually doing something, it allows us time to reflect, to relax and to formulate new plans for out life.

- Retirement requires planning. Just as one plans a vacation, so too must one plan their retirement.

- Must derive a sense of personal identity away from the occupation to feel useful.

- Deal with feelings of loss of control and power.

- Learn to cope with a spouse who is still employed.

- Retirement generally means reduced income. Typically the retiring firefighter must learn to reduce his level of spending and live according to his prevailing financial situation. In other words, watch the overspending which generally leads to more stress.

- The retiring firefighter must develop a new meaning and purpose each day, he must develop a balance in life.

- Begin to learn about one's self and develop hobbies, or renew an old hobby or interest. The most devastating aspect heard among many retirees is the idea of "killing time". We must remember as all times that life is time. When we kill time, we are killing a part of life.

- Devoting part of one's time to community, religious, or other activities which can help in several ways. First, it allows us to give something back to community and as importantly, it helps to take our mind off our own life situation.

- A primary way to overcome the despair of retirement is to communicate with another. Do not hold these feelings inside. They must be shared.

- Begin to socialize with other than fire related personnel. It is imperative that you do not isolate yourself with feelings of self pity and fantasies of the way things used to be.

In conclusion, we must always remember that retirement does not mean a closing of the book of life — just another chapter.

SUMMARY

RETIREMENT

For the occupationally injured firefighter in the midst of a disability retirement, the pressures and uncertainty, especially about the future, are great, and the fears enormous.

PSYCHOLOGICAL ISSUES RELATED TO RETIREMENT

- Feelings of inadequacy and low self worth

- Fear of loss of control

- Uncertainty about the future are felt by many new retirees

- Fears of isolation from society

- "How will society view me?"

- What does one do with their compulsive work habits upon retirement?

POINTERS FOR SURVIVING RETIREMENT

- Maintain a positive survival spirit

- Learn to live in the present

- Limit all additional life changes for a period of time, 6 months to one year

- Overcome the "Poor Me" attitude — this takes serious effort

- Overcome thoughts and resulting feelings of inadequacy and low self worth

- Learn to do nothing. Doing nothing is, in reality, doing something

- Plan for your retirement

- Derive a sense of personal identity away from the occupation

- Deal with feelings of loss of control and power

- Learn to cope with a spouse who is employed

- "Hunker-down" and live according to your current financial situation

- Watch the overspending, this generally leads to more stress

- Develop a new meaning and purpose each day

- Develop a balance in life

- Begin to learn about one's self

- Develop hobbies, or renew an old hobby or interest

- Devote part of one's time to community, religious, or other activities

- Communicate with others—do not hold feelings inside—they must be shared

- Begin to socialize with other than fire-related personnel

- Don't isolate yourself with feelings of self-pity or fantasies of what used to be

- Always remember that retirement does not mean a closing of the book of life—just another chapter

THE FIREFIGHTER BURNOUT SYNDROME

And one might therefore say of me that in this book I have only made up a bunch of other people's flowers, and that of my own I have only provided the string that ties them together.

Montaigne

There is little disagreement that firefighter work is, at times, highly stressful. However, clinical experience and the results of recent research indicate that stress, as manifested by members of the firefighter community, is due more to psychological factors than to potential physical dangers involved in firefighter work.

Job pressures, the responsibility of protecting the public, internal departmental conflicts, the maintenance of macho defenses, bipolar (good-bad) thinking, emotional distancing from others, poor diet, and lack of exercise to help discharge internal pressures are more emotionally, psychologically, and physically debilitating than the risk of being injured or killed while doing their job.

Stress is a part of everyday life. It is the interaction of our efforts to cope with the internal demands we place upon ourselves, and the external demands of our environment. Stress and its effects are cumulative, they add up. Burnout is the sum total of our efforts to cope with the stresses and frustrations in our life.

In the struggle to cope, there has been an increasing rise in the number of cases of "burnout." As we have seen, it is a syndrome of physical, psychological, and emotional exhaustion, cynicism, suppressed anger and despair that frequently occurs among individuals involved in public service-related jobs. These people deal with others who, like themselves, are under acute or chronic tension and stress. Firefighters are constantly dealing with individuals under less than favorable, or outright horrible, conditions. The individuals they deal with may be in a state of shock, crisis, physical trauma and injury, grieving, agitation, or other emotionally charged state.

Generally, a firefighter is the first to arrive at the scene of a crisis and the last to leave. Most often, his emotional and perceptual experience of the scene is intense and vivid, frequently reliving the scene over and over in his mind in order to file an "accurate" report about it later.

For the firefighter, the social expectation is that he suppress his emotions while doing his job. This begins to carry over to his personal life when the shift is over. In time, the psychological and emotional "baggage" becomes heavier and more difficult to carry around.

Many firefighters feel let down by the "system" which is not as supportive as they believe it should be. Firemen look to their chief as a symbolic "father" and other supervisors as part of their extended family. They maintain the belief that stress problems would be less prevalent if the administration exhibited more concern for their well-being. Additionally, many officers feel as though the department treats them as expendables when they become less productive, like a disposable lighter which has run out of fuel — discarded. These firemen come to feel disillusioned with their expectations of departmental support, which, when not met, leads to a sense of letdown. Also experienced is frustration with the system, those who run it, and the fact that things don't seem to change. As one paramedic stated, "Same shit, different day!"

As the process of burnout continues, firemen begin to feel more negative about their self-worth and worth to others. Physical exhaustion, susceptibility to disease, and psychologically based disorders such as ulcers, back problems, intense chest pains and headaches generally accompany the burnout condition. Alcohol use and abuse are employed by victims of stress as their means of self-medicating. This further contributes to low morale, impaired performance levels, absenteeism, and high turnover of personnel within a department. On the home front, the self-medicating firefighter frequently finds himself the subject of his family's anger, and their feelings related to a lack of family cohesiveness. This further adds to the condition of overload for the stressed-out firefighter.

A firefighter's attitude of right and wrong were formulated prior to his emplemployment. Being on a fire department vividly accentuates them. The firefighter's family bears the brunt of his bi-polar, "no gray" philosophy and becomes a major aspect of the firefighter's stress syndrome, often resulting in the acting out of one's frustrations at home. Suddenly, the prestige of being a member of a firefighter's family ceases to be important. Instead, it becomes a source of discomfort.

Due to his intimate familiarity with the most traumatic aspects of life, the firefighter allows no room for straying from the "straight and narrow" for his spouse or children. Yet he may find himself breaking the very code of morality to which he forces his family to adhere. There is frequently so great a discrepancy between what a firefighter sees and feels during the work shift and its relationship to his own personal life that the coping efforts can become exhausting for him.

The firefighter is reluctant to tell his family about his work in order to protect them from the everyday horrors experienced on the job. In reality, he is also protecting himself from reliving the situations and experiencing the stresses all over again. In so doing, the stress or tension becomes locked within himself. It begins its destructive work from the inside out, and the emotional distance between a burned-out firefighter and his family continues to widen as the burnout syndrome advances.

Family relationships often prove to be a pivotal point in diagnosing a burnout condition. An increase in marital and parent-child difficulties often points to problems on the job. The firefighter can't take off his internal pressure like he does his uniform; he gets tougher with his family and more rigid and dogmatic in his attitudes. His bipolar thinking about right and wrong becomes more prominent in his communication and behavior.

As a firefighter's stress worsens, he increasingly shuns social activities for solitary ones. This becomes his defense for survival. He sometimes correctly assumes that his off-duty contacts with people will be just as upsetting as his on-duty work. Consequently, the stressed-out firefighter's perception of reality becomes so distorted that he shuns his otherwise primary source of social and professional interaction — being with other firefighters. Burnout has taken over!

Burnout is a reality, and those in public service are becoming more aware of the ever-present danger of being consumed by the very system they are sworn to serve.

Fire Departments must avoid burnout at all cost. For costly it is, not only monetarily, due to a tremendous loss of trained and dedicated personnel, but costly from the emotional and psychological toll it takes on the burnout victim and those close to him.

Fire administrators must begin to approach the problem of stress management without stigma or prejudice, and with a sensitivity to the needs of all its employees. Problem areas must be identified and practical alternatives formulated to reduce stress factors at work.

The answer to the management of occupational stress and burnout is awareness, acceptance, and action by the fire administration and the employee. Stress is inevitable and treatable. *Burnout is a waste!*

A

B

D

R

Racial prejudice 30
Relaxation methods
    breathing exercises 78
    hypnosis 54
    Jacabson's Progressive Method 77
    meditation 78
    relaxation training 162
    relieve tension 77
    Systematic Desensitization 79
Resistance Stage
    defense mechanism 20-21, 44
    defined 20
Restlessness 42
Restructuring thoughts 74
Retirement
    and stress 185
    early 139
    pointers for surviving 188-190
Role expectations 8
Role of "victim" 48
Role of firefighter 29

S

Savior role 26
Self image 30
Self-Directed Approaches
    communication 47
    examine personal myths 49-50
    integrate grey areas 50
    lower self-expectations 48
    physical health 51
    resolution of stress 46
Self-disclosure 73
Self-fulfilling prophesy 88
Self-image 140